Wolfpack Ramblings

CONTENTS ▌

CONTENTS

CONTENTS

1

Groundhog Day is Like a Walk Around Campus

Faculty members, I once read, make their livings comparing things that don't need to be compared. Things like the similarities and differences between ant colonies and socialist governments. Or the creative principles of Andy Warhol as the basis for 20th Century land-use planning. Or, maybe, the wisdom of Jesse James as applied to retirement investing.

So let me tell you how Groundhog Day is like my thousand-mile walk across campus. Not Groundhog Day the day—February 2—but Groundhog Day the movie. *Groundhog Day* is my favorite movie of all time.

Here's a re-cap of the plot. A slacker weatherman (Murray) from Pittsburgh is dispatched to Punxsutawney, Pennsylvania, for the annual weather prediction by the most famous prognosticator of all, groundhog Phil. Murray detests covering this inane event. An unexpected storm causes the crew to stay in Punxsutawney a second night. When Murray awakens the next morning, to a clock-radio blasting, "I Got You Babe" by Sonny and Cher, it is February 2 again.

And so it continues, day after day after day; Harold Ramis, the writer, claimed the main character re-lived that one day 10,000 times. Murray evolves through the process in several hilarious stages, gradually getting to know the people of Punxsutawney. He eventually awakens to a new day (I'll not spoil the whole plot for you), but for our purpose, the relevant bit is that he admits he's been around for so long that he has seen a lot and, consequently, knows a lot.

There is always something happening on the NC State campus. This day it was Shack-A-Thon, featuring a nice "shack" put up by students in the College of Natural Resources.

Like Bill Murray walking around Punxsutawney, I walked around the NC State campus for a long time. About sixteen years. First as dean of the College of Natural Resources, with a relatively small radius around Biltmore and Jordan Halls. Then, as provost, with journeys almost every day that took me to the far reaches of campus. And then, beginning in 2009, as a faculty member again, walking to class and back. More importantly, after returning to the faculty, I started walking at lunch to get some exercise. Three miles at the least; when pushed by occasional walking buddy Dave Ranier, four or five. Since I retired in 2017, I only walk around campus occasionally, but the memories are still fresh.

So, let's estimate that after I returned to the faculty I walked 3 miles on average per day, 3 days per week and 40 weeks a year (leaving out times when I had a meeting, was out of town or the weather stunk). That's about 360 miles per year. Seven years at that rate, and the total distance is a shade over 2500 miles. But to be within the appropriate confidence limits, I'll just claim 1,000 miles of my Wolfpack ramblings.

Keep walking around the same place day after day and, just like Bill Murray in Punxsutawney, you see a lot. You notice the kind of things that others might miss on a forced march from lecture to lab or office to meeting, head down, legs pumping, brow furled and mind fixed on the task ahead. Trekking around campus with hat pulled down low, sunglasses on, earbuds in and reading the cellphone screen isn't a formula for enlightened observation.

But taking a stroll over lunch, just to get some fresh air and make your cardiologist happy, is. There's a lot to see on campus. You'll notice that a lot of the storm drains have fish forged onto them. You'll wonder about the patterns of yellow bricks on the sidewalk along Cates Drive. You'll move to the rhythm of the metallic pings of batting practice as you skirt the outfield of Doak Field. You'll discover that the first forsythia bushes to bloom in the spring (winter, really) are on Hillsborough along Caldwell Hall.

I learned to observe such things from my friend Charlie Leffler, now retired from being Vice Chancellor for Business and Finance, the university's CFO. Whenever we walked to a meeting together, he always made us take different routes, going and coming. That, Charlie said, let him keep an eye on campus. He'd make notes about a sidewalk that needed repair, a wall that needed paint, a tree that needed trimming. And he'd pick up trash that we encountered. Gotta love it when the CFO is policing the litter.

Chalk on the sidewalks is a favored form of communication!

Charlie concentrated on the physical condition of campus—that was part of his responsibility—but I was less focused (he would say I was always less focused, not just on our walks). And after I'd returned to the faculty, I was just out for a totally aimless walk-about. I'd share high-fives with students from my Conservation of Natural Resources course or study-abroad trips to London and Prague, answering their greetings of, "Hey, Uncle Larry!" I'd chat with faculty colleagues I hadn't seen for some time, some of whom still called me Mr. Provost. I'd read the messages chalked on the sidewalk or painted on the Free-Expression Tunnel, work on my mental map of where to find a block S imbedded in the bricks. And lots more.

Those observations and many others were the stimuli for writing the stories that comprise this book. But, of course, I've taken a lot of liberties with those stimuli to tell the stories I wanted to tell. You walk a thousand miles, you get some poetic license.

I've walked a lot farther than a thousand miles in my university life. I spent nine years on campus as a student, forty as an employee. Since I was eighteen, the only times I wasn't on campus were an Army tour of duty in Vietnam and one year on sabbatical at the Wisconsin Department of Natural Resources. My guess is that I've walked at least 10,000 miles during my nearly half-century of time at the Universities of Illinois, Missouri, Cornell, Virginia Tech, Penn State and NC State.

I've learned, lived and loved much from all the places I've walked, but never so much as at NC State. If you are a veteran of NC State, I hope you feel the same way that I do and that these stories will bring a smile. If you are anticipating rather than remembering NC State, I hope you'll walk many pleasant miles across our campus and live for yourself some of the experiences I've related. And if you are just a lover of universities, I hope my stories kindle some pleasant memories of your own.

In any case, take out the earbuds and pocket your phone. Take a stroll and take in your environment. Otherwise, like in *Groundhog Day*, you might just wake up tomorrow back in today.

2 ▌

First and Ten, Wolfpack Style

A student stopped me outside Withers Hall one day to ask an important question. He was nervous. "Are you the guy who announces the football games? Your voice sounds just like him."

"No," I answered, "And you just insulted an NC State living treasure." I also should have told him to get his ears checked. Or not drink so much at football games. Because I sound nothing like the PA announcer for NC State football.

Something magical happens at Carter-Finley whenever our team makes a first-and-ten. At that point, the public address announcer's voice crackles out over the stadium saying, with understated emotion, "And that's another Wolfpack..." and the fans all complete the sentence, thundering "...first down!"

The crowd is well trained, having learned the routine over the years from others in the stands, just like robins learn to eat earthworms from their older brothers. But how did such a tradition get started?

Dr. Edward Funkhouser started it, that's how. The living treasure who announced the NC State football games for nearly two decades is Ed Funkhouser, recently retired Emeritus Associate Professor of Communication. Over lunch one day, Ed told me the rest of the story.

Ed grew up in rural Virginia with a radio in his ear and in his heart. It is as simple as this: "I love being behind a microphone," he said. He's been behind one for most of his life. As a teenager, he hosted a sports show on a local radio station. "I wrote, produced and broadcast the entire show," he said. "I even sold the advertising." While in college getting three degrees—like many of us baby boomers, he was the first person in his family to get any degree, let alone three—he worked part-time for commercial and public radio stations in Virginia and Tennessee.

Ed Funkhouser in his natural habitat -- behind a
microphone!

He landed in Raleigh in 1977, as an assistant professor of communication. And he's been here ever since, teaching, advising and doing whatever administrative job needed doing. Throughout his 40 years at State, he was never far from a microphone.

Early in his NC State career, the director of the marching band, Don Adcock, asked him if he knew anyone who could announce for the band at football games.

"I suppose I could do it," said Ed. Adcock invited him over to Price Hall for an audition, handed him a megaphone and told him to talk—loud. Two minutes later, he had the job. Adcock wanted an announcer because he worried that the fans wouldn't be able to figure out the formations they were making on the field. Once, when the band formed up a spinning wheel to honor the textile program, the script read, "As you can clearly see,..."

Ed moved on to helping with the football games as a side-kick to another NC State institution—C. A. Dillon. Dillon announced Wolfpack basketball games for more than half a century—spanning the entire time the men's team played in Reynolds Coliseum, including the 1974 and 1983 national championship runs. He also did football, but in later years only wanted to announce the games themselves, not the pre-game and halftime festivities. That's where Ed came in, the salad and vegetables around Dillon's meat-and-potatoes announcing. Dillon worked the first men's basketball game when the RBC Center (now PNC Arena) opened in 1999, and then promptly retired from both basketball and football announcing. Ed grabbed the football microphone and didn't put it down until 2017.

Ed's work as a professor closely paralleled his work as an announcer. His specialty is mass communication, especially radio and television. His work in the community is legion. In 1983, he co-founded the Triangle Radio Reading Service, which records newspapers, magazines and books for the visually impaired. That, and other work that mixes theory and practice, earned him a place in NC State's Academy of Outstanding Extension Faculty.

Listening to Ed Funkhouser is like drinking fine wine—it goes down smooth, neither aggressive nor cloying. "If you are going to be good at this," he said, "You need to be scared each time you switch on the mike." What might seem effortless to listeners is actually the product of hard work and preparation. Ed started each game more than two hours before kick-off, meeting with the opponent's sports information director to get the pronunciation of their players' names correct. He worked with spotters who fed him the numbers of offensive players handling the ball and defensive players making the tackles. Good spotters are god-sends, he said, because they can focus on the details of the plays, and not get distracted cheering for the team. The concentration on the game is intense, and when he finally told the crowd goodbye and to "drive safely," he went home exhausted.

An element of communication theory was the key to Ed's now-famous phrase. He calls it para-language, the part of oral communication that goes beyond words. An example—the relevant one here—is "the pregnant pause," the temporary halt in a sentence that rivets the listener's attention. If a teacher wants to get a class' attention, he said, the best strategy is to stand up—and say nothing.

That's what he did on Saturday, October 9, 1999, when State played Clemson on national television. It was just his third game as the new permanent announcer. Ed wanted to see if he could get the crowd involved. So, the first time the Wolfpack passed the first-down marker, he announced over the loud-speaker, "And that's a Wolfpack..."—wait for it, wait for it, wait for it—"...first down!" A few more pregnant pauses on a few more first downs, and the crowd of

48,790 was into it big time, finishing his sentence every time. The Pack won, 35-31, and a tradition was born.

I can hear the crowd now: "And that's another NC State...first down!"

Where did he get the idea? East Carolina University says he stole it from them. Not true, according to Ed. He'd never heard an East Carolina game before then, but he's since heard their cheer; the PA announcer says "first down," and the crowd yells, "Pirates."

Nope, Ed says, he didn't parrot the Pirates, but based his phrase on the persona of NFL referee Red Cashion. Cashion was a huge man who motioned big when a team made a first down and accompanied it with a booming, "First down!" He was also inspired by major league umpire Dutch Rennert, who made a melodrama of calling balls and strikes. Today, teams all over the country have hopped on board. The New York Jets and Miami Dolphins do it, as well as many college teams. "I just wish I could figure out some way to make money from it," Ed lamented.

Don't worry about the money, Ed. Think about it this way. For the 18 years you called the game, NC State averaged 7 home games per year, and, according to the NCAA, a team makes an average of 20 first downs per game. So, while you were behind the microphone, the Wolfpack made 2380 first downs. With an average attendance of, say, 50,000 fans, about half of whom are paying attention at any time, that means you've been quoted over 60 million times. That legacy, as the commercial says, is priceless.

3

A Monster Ate My Building

How many times have you used a version of, "My dog ate my homework"? (my printer jammed, I forgot my password, my battery died, ...). And what percentage of the time was it math homework?

How fitting that I should be walking through the Brickyard one summer day in 2016 to watch a monster eat Harrelson Hall, the home of NC State's Mathematics Department for half a century.

Harrelson Hall towered over the southern edge of the Brickyard, looking like a wide, squat castle tower that lost its castle. It was a monument to what happens when function follows form, rather than the other way around. Harrelson was built in 1961, a renowned architectural masterpiece—the first round building on a university campus in the United States, maybe the world. It was said at the time to be the pinnacle of efficiency and beauty. It featured wedge-shaped classrooms, wider at the rear than at the front, pointing in toward the center of the building and sloping from the back to the front. Seemed like a good idea, focusing everyone's attention towards the sage on the stage.

Only two little problems. First, the sloping floors were just steep enough that a water bottle or Mountain Dew can accidentally dropped at the back of the room would roll all the way down to the feet of the instructor, an agonizingly slow and noisy journey. Second, the front of the room was convex. Consequently the black-boards (eventually, the whiteboards) at the front of the room were also convex. The website for the history of the math department used this feature as a geometry lesson:

> *The space occupied by a classroom in Harrelson Hall has the shape of an element of volume in cylindrical coordinates. A horizontal cross-section has the shape of an element of area in polar coordinates as shown in the figure below. The classrooms originally had curved blackboards so that a student at point A could not see past point B on the blackboard.*

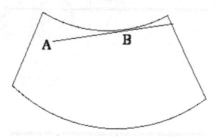

In other words, teachers couldn't teach in it and students couldn't learn in it. QED.

I taught a guest lecture in Harrelson once, just once. I think there were students around the corner from where I was standing, but I couldn't be sure. I do know they couldn't see the slides I was showing. Never went back again.

No one else ever wanted to go back again, either. Within a decade of opening, the building's innovative shape had turned from architectural inspiration to pedagogical hatred. The History Department, which shared the space with Math, described the building in 1972 as "one of the most unsatisfactory buildings imaginable."

Harrelson Hall during the "deconstruction"

But the real fatal flaw wasn't the nonsensical classrooms, but the nonsensical hallways. The building featured a spiral sloping corridor that ran from top to bottom, useful primarily for downhill grocery cart slaloms and skateboard derbies. The corridor eventually made the building obsolete. There was no way to make it meet ADA requirements. Elevators couldn't help—every room was still either uphill or downhill at an un-negotiable grade. In 2003, the university concluded the inevitable: Harrelson Hall had to go. Removal waited more than a decade, until the university's budget found room to raze this architectural innovation.

Three cheers for the university, however, as it embarked on a "deconstruction," rather than demolition. In a carefully staged multi-year process, virtually everything that could be salvaged was salvaged. Bit by bit, pieces were removed and repurposed. Audio-visual equipment went to other classrooms, whiteboards were donated to a new local high school, carpeting was re-used by the College of Education, old doors went to the fire department for training exercises and furniture went to Habitat for Humanity or surplus sales. Concrete blocks and other non-hazardous materials were shipped to recycling plants to be ground into gravel or otherwise deployed as construction material. In all 95% of the building was "salvaged, scrapped or recycled," according to the university's final project report, keeping 11 million pounds out of the landfill and providing $300,000 in value from re-used materials.

At the end, mechanical monsters chewed up what was left of Harrelson.

But the final stage was the best. The shell of the building stood gaunt and ghostly, windows and frames removed so that it looked like a 100-eyed skull. Huge mechanical monsters closed in on the gutted structure and starting eating it. Looking like evil transformers in a science-fiction movie, long-necked metal dragons bit hungrily into the floors and walls, massive jaws crunching away as if the building were a multi-story moon-pie. Along with a few dozen others, I watched, mesmerized, as the building disappeared, glutinous bite by glutinous bite. Rat-like front-end loaders gathered the final scraps. In a matter of days, the carcass was eaten completely.

And now the former building site is a beautiful, green plaza. A border of longleaf pines, looking like trees having a bad hair day, surround the plaza (don't worry, in a few years, they will be stunning). Mixed in with the grass and shrubs are a series of short vertical concrete panels, angled like radii, memorializing the failed interior plan of Harrelson Hall. Eventually another building will end up on the site, but for now the plaza is a green monument to being willing to admit our mistakes.

Next time your dog eats your homework, let's hope it works out this well.

4

Mulch Madness

Please finish this sentence: "It's spring, and a young man's fancy turns to ..."

The old-fashioned ending is "love."

The ending I grew up with is "baseball."

On tobacco road, the answer is "basketball." More specifically, the NCAA Final Four. March Madness.

But at NC State, the real madness in March is for mulch. Huge piles of the fragrant stuff appear, strewn around campus like not-so-ancient burial mounds. Crews of grounds workers fill the back-ends of miniature dump trucks and distribute it in smaller piles. Then bigger crews of workers with shovels and rakes spread it like the shaved toppings on a thousand coconut cream pies. Around trees, in flower gardens, on bare spots of clay that can't even grow weeds. The campus smells, uh, mulchy. Indeed, we go mad for mulch.

I have a love-hate relationship with mulch and its progenitor, leaves. Seems crazy to me that I spend fall weekends at home raking all the leaves in our natural areas into piles to be picked up at the curb. And then I spend the spring hauling bags of mulch from Lowes and spreading them around where the leaves used to be. But it looks so nice when the leaves are gone, and just as nice when the mulch is new and thick and smelly.

It's spring, and mounds of mulch appear across campus.

The NC State campus lives this paradox on a grander scale. In the fall, the same army of workers that spreads mulch in the spring is hard at work collecting leaves from around campus. Armed with blowers and rakes, they herd up the leaves like cattle drovers in the old West. Giddy-up, you dang-blasted maples! Stay in the pile there, you cussed oaks! Head-off that stampede of escaping sweetgums and hickories!

Is god laughing at us, or is there a purpose to this annual migration of organic material? To answer that question, I turned to NC State's mulch expert, Jeff Del Pinal, Program Manager for Grounds. Jeff has been here for several years now, up from Florida, and you can see his eyes gleam when the subject turns to gathering, grinding, composting and spreading.

So, here's the good news: NC State is pretty darn conscientious about how we take care of our grounds, working hard to be sustainable. We collect about 1 million pounds of leaves each year. That's enough to fill a football field three feet deep. All those leaves get transported to Raulston Arboretum, where they are composted and then used as mulch around their plantings. All the branches and wood chips from pruning trees go to the Department of Horticulture Sciences's Field Labs. They add leaves and other organic material, compost it up for awhile and we use it for mulch. That mulch isn't so pretty, though, so it goes into areas that aren't regularly visited on campus. Finally, the big bits—logs and large branches that can't be easily ground up in the kind of machines used in the movie *Fargo*—are sent to charitable organizations that use them for firewood or landscaping.

And if you add all our recycled mulch together, it still wouldn't be close to enough to meet our campus needs. Depending on the year, we spread about 700 cubic yards around campus—enough to cover a football field 5 inches deep. So, we still need to buy the usual triple-shredded hardwood mulch that looks so good and smells so good around my garden. But by the semi-load, not the bag. And despite how it seems to me—that we are drowning in mulch—not every square foot is mulched each spring. The campus is on a 2-3 year rotation, so the mulch doesn't get too thick and start to cause problems of its own.

But there's a mulch bigger story here. Our campus grounds program is awesome. Not only is our campus literally green, but it is philosophically green as well. Sustainability is all around us. Jeff says what attracted him here, and keeps him enthused, is that our landscaping is linked to our bigger purpose—learning and teaching. "It's about education and forward movement," he insists, not just about keeping the place looking spick-and-span.

Our campus is filled with surprising beauty, like this unexpected patch of daffodils in a small garden behind Fountain Dining Hall.

We've installed pollinator gardens around campus, so keeping bees and other pollinators healthy is part of Jeff's mission. Therefore, they've cut way down on using herbicides to control weeds. Instead, they spray "horticultural vinegar" on weeds, causing the plant cells to dehydrate and die (I checked—horticultural vinegar is 4-6 times more vinegar-y than the brands from the grocery store, so don't put it on your salad). We've installed over 140 passive storm-water devices around campus—such as the dry areas of grasses and rock berms outside behind Talley Student Center. The Grounds folks are working with students as part of "living labs," in which students help design, plant and maintain areas. The "Artist's Backyard" between Owens and Turlington residence halls is just one example. Other examples abound, from green roofs to electric riding mowers to using excess plants from construction projects to spruce up small areas elsewhere. Nothing is wasted, and nothing goes to the landfill.

The results are stunning. As an avid walker around campus, every day I see small places, hidden places, that are beautiful. An unexpected bed of flowers behind the brick retaining wall at Dan Allen and Hillsborough. A flowering magnolia at one of the Coliseum Deck entrances. A patch of daffodils next to the picnic shelter behind Fountain Dining Hall. A swing in the small patch of grass near the Free Expression Tunnel, surrounded by native grasses. From a campus described in college guides as one of the nation's ugliest twenty years ago, we've now got a campus that professional landscapers from other universities are visiting to get inspiration and guidance.

So, Shakespeare got it wrong. It's not much ado about nothing—it's mulch ado about something!

5

Goodbye, Bowling Alley

"You mean you've never been to the bowling alley?" Steve Keto asked me in shock.

"No," I answered. "Where's the bowling alley?"

Obviously, my education about NC State and Raleigh was badly lacking. Here I was, provost of the university, and I had no idea a bowling alley resided just across Hillsborough Street from D. H. Hill Library.

"I'm taking you there for lunch next Thursday," Steve insisted. "The best meatloaf in town."

And he was right. It was great meatloaf, with sides of peas and mashed potatoes. I'm pretty much an expert on meatloaf—it would be my choice for last meal—and this meatloaf was great. Sliced thick, sturdy enough to hang together, moist enough to ooze at the touch of a fork, brown gravy that made you remember grandma. The Thursday special was about the cheapest big helping of delicious comfort food to be found within a wolf's howl of campus. Unfortunately, meatloaf disappeared from the menu a few years ago, with the retirement of the cook, so the burger and fries—just as tasty—became my new favorite.

Steve and I started making it a regular occasion, on Thursdays when nothing else got in the way. As well as being a friend, Steve was the associate vice-chancellor for business and finance, and a guy who knew his way around a dollar bill. Steve went on to be Vice Chancellor for Finance and Operations at the University of Minnesota at Duluth before retiring last year. When we spoke by phone, he recalled the special care provided by the African-American cook and manager:

> *She worked there since the 1960s, before she could eat in the dining area. Her sister also cooked, and her son used to monitor the parking garage. In addition to meatloaf the breakfasts were the best in Raleigh - cheese omelet, hash browns, toast and coffee for about $4.00. I used to have my staff meetings there when I had the financial and IT folks reporting to me—probably about 15 folks. She would set up a special table for us, complete with tablecloth, and give us all separate checks. Can't get that service anywhere else these days.*

But, come on, a bowling alley across the street from campus? Wouldn't almost any other business—a tie-dye t-shirt shop, maybe—be more profitable than a bowling alley?

Apparently not, because a bowling alley had been on that site across from D.H. Hill since 1940. Before then, Hillsborough Street was lined with houses, not businesses. I suppose the big men on campus (that is, deans) lived there. But in 1939, construction of a new concept began—a strip shopping center. The following fall, the Manmur Bowling Center opened its doors with 24 gleaming maple bowling lanes. A staff of nine "pin boys" worked the lanes, resetting the pins after each roll of a bowling ball. The newspaper reported that the business hours were "9 a.m. until everyone is tired."

The new Manmur Bowling Center also featured adjacent business sites for a shoe shop, barber shop, beauty shop, soda fountain, restaurant and grocery store. This was uptown!

Until 1959, that is, when a massive fire took out the whole block. About 200 people were in the building when the fire was discovered, but they all escaped unharmed. NC State students poured out of their dorms to watch the city's entire fire department fight the blaze for several hours. Someone observed that if Chancellor Caldwell wanted to address the entire student body, then would have been his best opportunity.

Within a year, the bowling alley was back. In 1960, the new alley opened as Western Lanes, the same 24 lanes, but this time with automatic pin-setting machines. The Manmur shoe shop and barber shop relocated a couple of blocks west—where they still operate today. (Manmur, if you are wondering, is a combination of Manteo and Murphy, the two geographic ends of North Carolina along U.S. Highway 64, which then ran right down Hillsborough Street).

The bowling alley had a special meaning to NC State. It was the "classroom" for PE 243, Bowling. And for 35 years, the one and only "professor of bowling" has been Henry Kidd. We met for lunch to reminisce about the good old days.

"The students call me Coach K," he told me. "I'm the original Coach K, not that imposter in Durham."

We did some math together. He'd been teaching bowling for 35 years, 2 semesters per year, 2 or 3 sections per semester and 32 bowlers per section. Add in summer classes, and he's taught about 6,000 NC State students howto bowl. Maybe a few less than that, because some students couldn't get enough. "One fellow took bowling eight times, and a female student took it seven times." Why in the world would someone do that?

That's when Henry got animated. "Some students take bowling because they don't like to sweat, some because it fits their schedule. But some just really love bowling." It was a diversion from academic life, especially because it happened across the street from campus. Most students in his classes in recent years have been freshmen, and, Henry said, they seemed particularly appreciative of a little down time.

And they liked the bowling course because they conquered something that seemed out of their reach. "Bowling is about life lessons," Henry said, "taking a challenge and succeeding." Or not. For example, when each Thanksgiving rolled around, he gave extra credit if a student bowled a turkey (three strikes in a row, remember?). "But they have to call me over before attempting their third strike, so I can watch. That gets them out of their rhythm, and me watching makes them nervous." Not very fair, I ventured. "Yep, that's the life lesson," smiled Henry.

I asked if teaching bowling is common on campuses like ours. Henry assured me it was, that many universities have bowling alleys in their student unions (I spent many happy hours at the University of Illinois' bowling alley during my undergraduate years, getting a little down time where a nerd like me wouldn't be out of place). When Talley Student Center was built in 1970, there were plans to put bowling lanes in the basement. But the bowling alley owners came to the university with a permanent discount for bowling students if we didn't build our own facilities that competed with theirs.

And so, for as long as anyone can remember, the bowling alley cranked out PE credits and dished up comfort food. Until November 26, 2016, that is, another day that will live in infamy. The bowling alley closed. The rumble of bowling balls silenced forever. The frustration of a 7-10 split vanquished. The joy of a pin-crushing strike gone. The tantalizing wobble of the last pin as it decides to fall or stand—well, we'll just never know.

And what has replaced it? A Target department store. And I'll bet they aren't serving meatloaf.

6

A River Runs Through It

Campus streams are often memorable for young, impressionable minds. That certainly was the case in the early winter of 1969, when I arranged to meet a young lady on the "banks of the Boneyard," the tiny stream that runs through the University of Illinois campus. A gentle snowfall had transformed the scene from a neighborhood of utilitarian engineering buildings to a Currier-and-Ives painting. The moment was magical, and the magic is still alive, a half-century later.

The campus stream at NC State had a similar, though less romantic, effect on Barbara Doll. One day, during her master's program, she was walking on campus and observed the stream where it passed near the university's motor pool. It was a Friday, and the motor pool staff was washing their fleet. Water and soap ran down the sloping parking lot into the storm drain that outfalls to the stream. Suds from the soap were head-high along the banks of the stream. As she walked downstream toward the baseball stadium, she found children playing in the polluted stream and the suds. Something clicked for Barbara Doll—she had to fix this mess.

"What campus stream?" you ask. Didn't know that our campus has a stream running through it? That's probably because you are running through campus yourself, crossing Rocky Branch Creek several times each day without realizing what's under your feet.

Rocky Branch Creek runs downstream from west to east across campus, roughly parallel to the railroad track. It passes along Sullivan Drive—past the motor pool where Barbara first encountered the suds—follows along between Miller Fields and the Carmichael Gym complex, and then continues along the southern edge of Dail Softball Stadium and Paul Derr Track and Soccer Field before entering Pullen Park.

A greenway accompanies the stream today, and the corridor is beautiful (even if still pretty well ignored by most people). That wasn't the case in the early 1990s. The state's environmental department had judged Rocky Branch Creek to be one of the most polluted streams in North Carolina. Almost nothing lived in the water. Barbara remembered seeing the stream running white from the line painting on athletic fields. The motor pool dumped used oil into the stream, and lots of pipes from unknown origins emptied surreptitiously along the banks.

Barbara is an extension associate professor in the Department of Biological and Agricultural Engineering. As a master's student and later as a university employee, she started bothering people around campus about the stream's condition. She found partners here and there—in facilities, the architect's office, some faculty members—and she helped form the Rocky Branch Committee in 1994. But she also found resistance—why were she and her colleagues worried about this trickle of water? It was just a drainage ditch.

"Everything had its back to the stream," she recalled as we shared lunch. The back-side of buildings abutted the stream, so that's where you put the dumpsters and the piles of broken equipment and left-over materials. Who knows, Jimmy Hoffa might have been buried back there.

As an extension specialist working on water quality issues, Barbara had a perfect opportunity to lead a restoration effort. Stream restoration was an emerging discipline, the state had just created the Clean Water Management Trust Fund, the clean-up of the Neuse River had gone into full gear (Rocky Branch Creek flows to the Neuse River, as does the rest of campus; check the man-hole covers) and her program needed a demonstration project to showcase what could be done. "I went after it like a pit bull," she said. "I sunk my teeth into it and didn't let go."

Working in partnership with the university's facilities program, she submitted several small grants to tidy up one problem or another. Then, in 1997, she hit the jackpot with a $1 million grant from the state's Clean Water Management Trust Fund. The restoration went from the minors to the big leagues. In three phases, the entire length of Rocky Branch Creek on campus has been restored.

The first stage was the westernmost, from Gorman Street to Dan Allen Drive. I arrived on campus in 2001, midway through this process. After years of erosion, the stream in cross-section resembled a V, with soil regularly flowing down to fill the bottom. Under the grant, bulldozers had begun reshaping it into a broad U that incorporated a small channel with a floodplain to spread and slow water during high flow, the profile for a properly functioning stream. Campus was of two minds. Some endorsed the project as a symbol of caring for the earth, especially our local earth. Some disparaged the work—ugly, they said, and totally unnatural, the shore stripped bare of vegetation and heavy equipment mucking around in the stream-bed.

But within a couple of years, it was beautiful again. The vegetation is back, so much so that some thinning has become necessary so walkers along the greenway can actually see the water. The stream gurgles its way, flowing faster where rock barriers narrow the channel, pooling up where small rock dams check the flow.

A small waterfall graces Rocky Branch Creek near where
it flows under Pullen Road on the eastern edge of
campus.

Phases two and three finished out the restoration by 2010—a full decade of work. In total, Barbara and her colleagues amassed $8 million for the entire project. "I just kept writing grants," she said. When it was all done, they had spent all but 32 cents.

Are you pleased with the outcome, I asked. Barbara nodded enthusiastically. Water quality has improved, and birds and wild mammals use the stream-side as high-quality habitat. Roland Kays, who teaches mammalogy in the Department of Forest and Environmental Resources, had students set up "camera-traps" along the stream for a class project (camera-traps take remote-triggered photos whenever they detect movement). His students photographed "a ton of raccoons and some opossums." They also captured an occasional white-tailed deer, coyote, fox and rabbit. Not a biodiversity hot-spot, perhaps, but also not a concrete jungle.

Most importantly, the campus no longer turns its back on the stream. The Athletic Department has helped develop a gateway where the stream-side path passes under Morrill Drive. The greenway that runs between there and Pullen Road is a favorite pathway for walkers and joggers—I'm seldom alone on my noon-time walks there. The City of Raleigh has awarded the project twice for environmental stewardship. Other universities call Barbara regularly to ask how they were able to accomplish such a major restoration. But the real measure of success? Barbara said, "I knew we were successful when I had a class out doing a project on the stream and we ran into two other classes doing their own field projects."

But I have my own definition of success. I hope that many times in the future, young couples will meet on the "banks of Rocky Branch," and their lives will change forever, too.

I was walking up Dan Allen one spring day when two students from Parks, Recreation and Sport Management approached from the other direction. One, who had taken my class, called the familiar, "Hi, Uncle Larry!" He was carrying a disgusting looking soccer ball. "Where'd you get that?" I asked. "From Rocky Branch," he answered. "We've been cleaning up the creek." He then opened his backpack to show me the whole catch—one soccer ball, one baseball, one basketball, one softball and 25 tennis balls! I trusted his tally, because the previous week I had walked the path that winds along the creek behind the tennis courts. A few feet along the courts, I started to notice the presence of day-glo yellow objects along the stream. Tennis balls! So I backtracked to the start of the border with the tennis courts and continued downstream, counting. I tallied 34 tennis balls.

"What are you going to do with them?" I asked.

"All my friends have big dogs that just love to chase and chew tennis balls," he answered.

Now that's recycling!

7

Marching to Our Own Tune

The knock on the door was assertive. No, it was aggressive. I knew I should pretend not to be there. Nothing positive was attached to the fist making that knock.

"Come in," I said, swallowing good sense in favor of being a responsible dean.

An irate faculty member advanced on my desk.

"You have to make them stop!" he demanded.

"Stop who from doing what?" I asked, confused because, in a faculty member's mind, there were so many possibilities.

"Them," he repeated and pointed out the window. "Them, the marching band. I can't concentrate on my work. They're driving me crazy."

It was mid-August, and the NC State Marching Band was making music on the field behind Biltmore Hall. The band's practice area had just been relocated from the Method Road soccer fields, where they had drilled for decades.

"I like it," I countered. "So just go back to your office and ignore them. It's only a few months until Christmas when the football season ends."

"Bah humbug." He stormed out, and the marching band kept marching outside our offices.

At a lunch meeting at 1887 in Talley, I asked Paul Garcia, NC State's Director of Bands and specifically Director of the Marching Band, if he gets a lot of complaints like this. He admitted that he gets the occasional irate message from a faculty member disturbed by their practices. But, he said, he gets maybe six positive comments for every negative one.

Paul said, "They tell me it reminds them that the new academic year has started." The first robins and daffodils signal the beginning of spring, and the first oompahs of the sousaphones and bangings of the snare drums signal the beginning of fall.

My appreciation is about the same, some good, some not so good. As a boy in Chicago, I lived across from Taft High School's athletic fields. In summer, the community drum and bugle corps practiced there on most weeknights. Before the comfort of air conditioning isolated people in their houses, my folks and I sat on the front steps, hoping for a breeze and listening as the band thumped out "Toot, toot, tootsie, good-bye, toot, toot, tootsie, don't cry." Good memory.

Then, as a college junior, I roomed with a member of one of those drum and bugle corps. He'd listen to marching-band albums on the record player for hours on end, drumming with his fingers on his desk for hours and making trumpet sounds through his lips. Not such a good memory.

When I led Penn State through a series of events to commemorate the October 12, 1999, date on which the earth's human population was said to have hit 6 billion people, I enlisted the Penn State Marching Band. At half-time of our game with THE Ohio State University (which we won), the band spelled out "6,000,000,000" on the field and played "It's a Small World After All." Great memory.

The Power Sound of the South performs at an NC State football game at Carter-Finley Stadium.

The NC State marching band is called "The Power Sound of the South." I always figured that it was because they were loud. They always sounded really loud to me. I've been at indoor alumni events when a subset of the band came into a small banquet room playing the fight song. Loud doesn't describe it. Are we particularly loud, I asked Paul, do we have more tubas and fewer piccolos than other bands, are we bigger than other bands? Is that why we're the "power sound"? He disappointed me on all questions. We're about average in size, at just over 300 members, and our instrumentation is typical. So why are we the power sound band?

"I don't really know," said Paul. "Most bands have a nickname of some kind. Gives them a persona, a presence. We picked 'Power Sound of the South' long before me, and it has stuck." Kind of like being THE Ohio State University (to differentiate them from other Ohio State Universities).

Marching bands are as American as apple pie, and the NC State Marching Band is almost as old as apple pie. Soon after the university began, a group of students asked to form a marching band, not to accompany football games, but to accompany military parades. That origin, Paul said, is a reason the NC State uniform still has a slightly military style, with a decidedly military hat—"an homage to tradition." Much later, the band got adult leadership and began playing for football games.

And, today, they play all over the campus and the world. According to Paul, the band is one of the most recognizable symbols of the university. Whether they are belting out the fight song at alumni gatherings around the state, playing the National Anthem at Martinsville Speedway, or representing the U.S. at parades in Spain, the name of North Carolina State University—excuse me, THE North Carolina State University—is spread far and wide.

And just how does all that music and marching get accomplished? Paul wants the band to have fun and "ownership," so he encourages his student musicians to suggest the songs and themes for half-time shows. "We play a lot of different music—more than most bands," he said. Our band feels sorry for their counterparts at Florida State, playing that same tomahawk chopping phrase over and over (I feel sorry for us, having to listen to the disgusting thing). "One game they counted—the Florida State band played that chant 54 times."

And just as you'd expect at a STEM school like State, Paul arranges it all using a computer program. He sets the starting position of the band and then the next position they want to form, and the program moves each musician—all 300+ of them—around the field. It isn't that easy, though, because Paul has to review it all to be sure that people aren't running into each other and can get from one place to another in the allotted time and number of steps. And he has to watch out that the band doesn't accidentally make any obscene pictures as they are moving around.

Paul said that students love being part of the band. Because we don't have a music major, our band is composed of students from all across the university who volunteer to march to Paul Garcia's drum beat. I decided to check his claim.

When it isn't football season, a portion of the marching band–the Pep Band– blasts out the tunes at basketball games.

My colleague in the College of Natural Resources, Jennifer Viets, was a band member during her undergraduate years in the early ninety's. Did she love it? "Being in the band absolutely made college for me," she said, her face lighting up like it was her birthday. It reduced a big school to a small group where she could belong. The band members came from everywhere—all disciplines, races, ethnicities, backgrounds—so the experience was truly the university in miniature. The members knew each other, supported each other, became a family of sorts. Jennifer said it was "an absolute blast. I don't remember a lot about other things during college, but I remember every road trip we took as a band."

Jennifer became a field conductor, which is called a drum major today. She was only the third female field conductor in NC State's history, the other two preceding her only a few years earlier. "All three were Jennifers, and all three were brunettes." She recalled the final game when then-band-director "Doc Hammond" was retiring. Rather than perform the program he had created, the band developed and played an alternative honoring him. He was dismayed at first, but once he relaxed, he enjoyed the recognition. "I'm lucky to have escaped with my diploma," Jennifer laughed, her face lighting up even brighter.

So, THE Power Sound of the South is powered by a source of energy that is truly renewable—the love of students for their school, their music and their friends. Jennifer summed it up this way: "You've got to find one thing to do at school. If you play an instrument, join the marching band. You'll love it."

And if you are a grumpy old faculty member who doesn't like to hear the band practice, all I can say is toot, toot, tootsie, goodbye.

8

Cinder-Block Heaven

Our older daughter, Jennifer (yes another one) recently returned to graduate school. After finishing one career in museums, she was heading for a second career as a speech-language pathologist. Most of the work could be done on-line, at home in El Paso, but the program required one semester in residence. So, she kissed her husband goodbye and headed up to the campus of Eastern New Mexico University in Portales. She signed up for the cheapest living option—married student housing. She texted pictures of her apartment complex with the caption, "Back to the post-war era!"

She had landed in a spot found on most public universities—a series of cinder-block low-rise apartment buildings on the outskirts of campus. Some were built after World War II and more after the Korean War to house the tidal wave of returning veterans taking advantage of the GI Bill. Our country promised veterans a good life after their sacrifices, and a free college education was part of the deal.

This new breed of students needed someplace to live, and sharing a dormitory with 18-year-olds fresh out of high school wasn't the answer. Nearly one-quarter of NC State's students in those days were veterans—usually married and often with children. Something more family-friendly was in order.

At NC State, we addressed the housing need by building E. S. King Village. Back in 1960, when it opened, the location on the western side of Method Road was on the edge of the university's footprint. It was out of sight from the rest of campus. The complex began life as the "Married Student Housing Development," but was re-named in the 1970s to honor Edward S. King, longtime director of the Raleigh YMCA and a fervent supporter of veterans and their families. The university constructed a community of 295 apartments spread among 17 buildings.

An NC State students waves to his wife and children at King Village in 1960, soon after it opened.

King Village was the height of what decorators and antique dealers have now nostalgically labelled "mid-century modern." No space and no materials were wasted. Plain lines, no decoration, just neat and tidy. The walls were cinder blocks—a mixture of cement and sand or rock. The ceilings were the same materials, formed into long narrow pre-cast panels. On the inside, the cinder-blocks were painted, on the outside they were faced with bricks (of course!). Closets, storage shelves and kitchen cabinets were wooden, shoehorned into the rooms to use all available space. Spartan, to be sure, but new, modern, roomy and efficient.

Whenever I pass through King Village on my walks around campus, I'm reminded of my own days as a graduate student at the University of Missouri. I was also a veteran, returning for a Master's degree after a tour in Vietnam. Sharon and I had been married for two years, expecting our first child at Christmas. We stayed in married-student housing—with the inspiring name of "Apartment Heights"—that looked remarkably like King Village.

Apartment Heights served us well. It was spartan, but also inexpensive, with plenty of room for our few belongings. Odd little cabinets that fit well into the kitchen or bedroom were handed down from graduating families to incoming ones. Playmates for kids and adults were plentiful and interesting. Aesthetics, however, were lacking. Cinder-blocks and bricks, dandelions and clover. I often said in those days that when I hit the lottery I was going to endow some trees for the playground. Nuts with scholarships, we needed some shade!

But that was 1972, nearly half a century ago. Things have changed. Returning veterans are fewer and perhaps unmarried or without children. Students in general want more for their housing dollar than spartan and efficient. They want Wolf Village—private bedrooms, air-conditioning, unlimited broadband, an outdoor plaza with covered seating.

So why, I wondered, would a big-time school like NC State, that was building new state-of-the-art residence complexes catering to 21st Century students, hang onto a time-worn anachronism like E.S. King Village? To get the answer, I invited Tim Luckadoo to lunch. Tim retired in 2016 as Vice-Provost for Campus Life, completing 24 years as the director of campus housing. Tim's answer was surprising, in many ways.

The first surprise was that Tim actually lived in King Village when he arrived on campus in the fall of 1992. He and his family spent six weeks there while waiting for their home to become available. "Our kids loved it," he remembered, because there were so many playmates from so many different places. "The door would fly open and twelve kids would come running in, speaking twelve different languages." After they moved, he still brought his children back on weekends to play with their friends.

From the days when the apartments were filled with U.S. veterans, King Village has transformed into an international community. The vast majority of residents—Tim guessed about 90%—are graduate students and their families from around the world. They like King Village because it is a no-frills affordable option for students on truly limited budgets—international students think like returning soldiers in the 50s and 60s. "King Village is safe, the apartments are roomy, the rent is low and there is lots of open space with great playgrounds," said Tim. Garden plots are even available if residents want to grow their own food.

Which led to my second surprise—King Village is at or near its rental capacity now all the time. When I arrived at NC State in 2001 and in the first years I was provost, occupancy was low. Tim confirmed that only about half the units were rented in those years, and the university was wondering what to do. Many other public universities, Tim said, had abandoned their equivalents of King Village, bulldozing the buildings or selling them, because the expense of keeping them up was breaking the budget.

The outside of the apartments at E. S. King Village look much like they did 60 years ago, but the insides are much improved, and students still love them.

NC State, I'm proud to say, made the opposite decision. We chose to invest rather than abandon. The big risk, Tim said, was our decision to build a community center in the midst of the complex, a capital investment that wouldn't directly increase revenue. Quality of life would improve, and we hoped higher occupancy would follow. And it worked. The residents love the center, which is always buzzing with activity—English-language classes, cooking and sewing workshops, kid's birthday parties, meetings of the Residents' Council (the residents have never been shy about asking for improvements, Tim said). Occupancy steadily increased over time, and King Village is again a going concern.

My third surprise was how much we've invested in the property over time. In truth, the place looks a bit shabby—"like an old army barracks, maybe," said Tim. My first idea for this story had been to compare King Village with Wolf Village across the street and tsk-tsk about how we weren't taking care of our international graduate students and their families. But shame on me for judging a community based on its cover.

The reality is that most improvements have been on the inside. The university has poured millions into King Village to make it safer and more comfortable, upgrades like double-pane windows, new sewage systems, sprinklers for fire protection, window air-conditioners, new banisters to replace those with buried layers of lead paint. The commercial-style flat roofs have been replaced by more homey looking peaked roofs; future installation of new furnaces and central air-conditioning in the attic space is in the plans. "It's more of a Volkswagen than a Cadillac," said Tim, but that's what the residents want—affordable utility rather than expensive amenities.

My last surprise was the names of the apartment buildings. Each building carries a letter (a humongous letter, readable from outer space), but also the name of a North Carolina county—Onslow, Jones, Hyde and 14 more, all in the coastal plain. I assumed the county names came first, when the apartments were full of veterans who might identify with them, and the letters came later, to make it easier for international students who might have trouble saying, let alone remembering, that they lived in Perquimans Building.

But no, the letters came first and were the only identifiers for 40 years or so. Early in Tim's tenure, a university edict came down saying that all campus buildings needed names. So the names were added, but the big letters stayed put. Everyone ignores the county names—campus police, maintenance workers, the community's office staff and the residents. As far as they are concerned, a window that needs to be fixed is in Building H, not Perquimans!

I understand King Village a lot more now, and I'm glad that we still have it. Maybe I'm even glad that it isn't all glitzy and modern, with statues of wolves and Block-S's imbedded in the sidewalk, like at Wolf Village across the street. King Village serves a very important purpose, by creating a community for international families. I drive by now and smile, watching kids on the playground, adults hanging laundry out to dry, people from anywhere and everywhere finding opportunity and a home at NC State. A university thrives on its diversity, and diversity in housing is just as relevant as all the other kinds.

As Tim said, "I have always had a special affinity for the place. At base level, you know, King Village is why we're here." It's just a little piece of cinder-block heaven right here on earth.

9

How Many Professors Does it Take...?

"How many professors does it take to change a light bulb?" The answer, of course, depends on whom you ask.

The legislature: "Fewer than we have now, and they shouldn't make so much money."

A departmental staff member: "(suppressed giggle)"

Students: "Will that be on the test?"

And faculty members themselves: "Change?"

Faculty members don't like change. We like to suggest that other things change—that, after all, is what our scholarship is all about, finding out new things that will change views of art, history, science, music, technology, climate patterns, whatever.

But change ourselves or what we do or how we do it—not likely. Ask a faculty member her favorite Broadway show tune, and I'll bet she'd raise her arms, twirl around and begin singing "Tradition" from *Fiddler on the Roof*. The academy is the bastion of tradition (for example, it's a place where people refer to themselves as "the academy" and use words like "bastion").

I ran into the buzz-saw of tradition regularly as provost. I'm an idea guy, and ideas lead to change. Faculty members don't like change. They particularly don't like change that affects them directly. Like when I agreed to implement a new way to collect student opinions of their teachers.

We had always done teacher and class evaluation with paper forms, handed out by faculty members in class, along with those dinky eraser-less pencils used to record putt-putt golf scores. We had lots of rules for how this should be done, such as avoiding the last day of class, making the faculty member leave after passing out the forms, having a trusted student collect the forms and return them to the departmental office in a sealed envelope, prohibiting faculty from treating students to cookies or candy on evaluation day. Most faculty members followed those rules, more or less, although some violated them in spades.

But that wasn't the issue for me. The issue was that months passed before the compiled surveys and comments were returned to faculty members for their use—you know, to improve teaching the next term. By the time we got the data back, though, the next term was in full swing and most of us can't remember what we did last week, let alone last semester.

So, being a STEM university, we decided that we might just use some of that stem stuff for ourselves. We decided to implement an online evaluation system, which we called ClassEval. For a couple of weeks at the end of the term, a website would be open on which students could complete electronic evaluations of their teachers and courses. The benefit: We could get the results back almost immediately after the final grades were in, and faculty members wouldn't have to mess with the forms, pencils and thick manilla envelopes that invited, oh, just a little peak. In other words, the evaluations would be done to provide almost "real-time" feedback with as little work as possible and no intimidation of the witnesses. A slam-dunk, I thought.

This is what filling out student evaluation forms used to look like.

Ah, tradition! The hated system of passing out forms, leaving the room and waiting months for the results suddenly became beloved! The new system represented change—the enemy of our bastion. Infidels at the palace gate! Storm troopers assaulting Luke Skywalker! A Trojan horse hiding an army of Millennial device-users!

Faculty outrage rapidly scaled up to DEFCON 1. Being good at criticism (that's what faculty members do to each other), they launched an armada of doubt about this so-called improvement. Would students actually do the evaluations? Would students be sober when they did them? What kind of response rates would we get? How would the results match up to the old style? Would students act like Chicago democrats, voting many times? And on and on and on.

It's been over a decade since we ousted those wonderful paper forms and instituted that ignominious website. I'm happy to report that we have survived, even thrived, under the new system.

To gather some actual data, I spoke with Grae Desmond, the guru of ClassEval, the guy who runs the program for the university's Office of Institutional Strategy and Analysis. How's it going? Real well, he said. Happily, he reported that we don't get complaints anymore from faculty members. Online evaluations have become the industry standard in universities now, so there really isn't any alternative.

Here's a snapshot of how ClassEval has worked, from a study done for Spring semester, 2017. A total of 131,334 student surveys were possible. Students completed 61,246 of them, or 46.6%. So, they do fill them out. That percentage is pretty stable from semester to semester, according to Grae.

Were students sober when they gave grades to teachers? I think so. On a typical day, only about 4% of the responses came in between 11 PM and 8 AM. That means 96% were sent when most students are still operating in full control of their senses. The peak time for completing surveys was 11 AM to noon; one-eighth of all surveys were done during that one hour. Two-thirds were completed in the 5-hour block between 10 AM and 3 PM, when students are most focused on their classes. Moreover, the average ranking given to teachers by students didn't vary a bit by time of day. So, sober or not, students know how they feel!

How did the electronic responses compare to those submitted on paper survey forms? The university's Office of Planning and Analysis did a study in 2008, soon after the new system was implemented, to test various aspects of the web-based process. Their basic finding was that, yes, they work. They compared response rates for paper-based and web-based systems for a subset of classes and found

66% for paper and 62% for online—not a statistically significant difference. They looked at average scores for the same instructor in different sections with paper and online systems; they were almost identical (4.25 versus 4.34, respectively), also not statistically significant.

And here's a not-surprising result: More serious students responded more often. Students getting higher grades, taking more hours, and enrolled in higher-level classes completed more surveys, as did women and graduate students. That means the quality and thoughtfulness of the responses is better for online than for paper surveys.

So, here we are, a decade after implementing a little change that produced great angst but has made the course evaluation system—and, we hope, teaching—much better. And no one is even complaining anymore. Which, perhaps, answers the question, "How many professors does it take to change a light bulb?" Only one, but it takes him ten years to do it!

10

The Library of WOW

The first time I saw Hunt Library, I whispered, "wow." I was peering cautiously over the edge of a big, deep rectangular hole in the ground. Well, you might say, all buildings start out as holes in the ground. But believe me, this was one gigantic hole—the Grand Canyon of university construction sites.

The journey to that big hole in the ground wasn't quick or easy. As the calendar marched into the new millennium, NC State's library situation was pitiful. We had great library staff and leaders, without question, and lots of books and journals, but our facilities were so last century. In terms of library space per student (a calculation that matters to accrediting agencies), we were the lowest among all the University of North Carolina system schools. And the situation for books was equally dire—with every new book that arrived, an older book was exiled into storage. First we filled up a building on Sullivan Drive, then moved on to a leased warehouse across the Beltline. In other words, D. H. Hill was not a fit space for students or books.

So, we put a new library on the list of capital projects for the university. Susan Nutter, our late and renowned Director of Libraries, and I, as provost, were the library's de facto champions. Getting the library on the list was easy, getting off it at the top end with a new building wasn't. Which projects move from good ideas to steel, concrete and brick is a political as much as a logical process. In order to advance in the new building game, you need some powerful friends. Engineering has powerful friends, and the result is obvious around the Oval on Centennial Campus—a small village of new buildings and more coming. Agriculture and science—the subjects we're known for—also have wealthy and powerful alumni and donors. The library isn't so lucky. It doesn't have political friends or well-healed alumni, and it doesn't field a football team. Quidditch, maybe, but not football.

When a new library finally elbowed its way to the top of the priority list, we celebrated. Prematurely, it turned out. A new teaching hospital for the College of Veterinary Medicine was in second place, and they were tired of waiting, too. Over the years university veterinarians had nursed the beloved pets of many a wealthy and powerful animal lover—and now they came to the rescue. A donor gave half the cost of the new building, and, whoosh, vet medicine vaulted over the library like a golden retriever jumping for a Frisbee!

The next year I was determined that nothing was going to butt in line ahead of the library. The chancellor agreed, so we made it. We named the proposed library after former Governor Jim Hunt, guaranteeing a politically powerful and popular ally. The General Assembly appropriated $120 million, and our new library was on the way.

I was appointed chair of the building committee, the happiest building project of my career. I had shepherded several other building projects at other universities and here—Jordan Hall addition, University College Commons, Bio-manufacturing Center, the Carroll Joiner Visitor Center, a vastly over-engineered forestry biotechnology greenhouse, part of the university golf course—but the new library was my baby.

The Hunt Library on Centennial Campus is truly the
library of WOW!

We were going to do this one right. From the beginning, the goal
was to create a new architectural icon for our campus. Not another
cereal box in red brick trimmed in grey metal. Not another building
that matched the "architectural design standards" of the university,
respectable, low-cost, and, to be honest, yawn-inducing. We wanted
something special, unique, stunning—and stunningly functional.

And we got it. By any measure, Hunt Library is the definition
of "WOW!" In partnership with a highly respected local architect,
we hired a world-famous architectural firm, Snøhetta, with offices in
New York and Oslo, that had fashioned some of the coolest buildings in modern times. They designed the new Library at Alexandria
(replacing the ancient one), looking like a giant sun dial lying aslant
on the ground, and the Oslo Opera House, resembling a glacier

melting into a fjord (it actually extends underwater). Unlike many famous architects, who develop a distinctive style that they build over and over regardless of the client, Snøhetta fits their designs into the owner's persona.

The library's persona is illustrated in the outrageous furnishings, including this freeform bench in the lobby.

As they got to know us, Snøhetta's architects gleefully discarded the idea of an x-story building. Instead, they envisioned a structure replicating a woven fabric, to represent our world-leading College of Textiles (across the street from the library site) and our mantra of integrating knowledge across disciplines to address society's problems. One floor would merge into another, with open spaces that connected across floors and functions. That's why, from the outside, you can't count how many floors the library has. And why the inside is a maze of different sized and shaped spaces for different functions and purposes. And why there are 80 different styles of chairs and couches that could have sprung from the pages of a Dr. Seuss book.

Of course not all the news along the way was good. The budget shrunk, as budgets always do, down to a meager $100 million (he wrote facetiously). Normally a deficit of that size would start several rounds of "value engineering." That basically means all the "wow" gets taken out of the building in order to maintain its original square-footage. Not this time, though. I insisted that we sacrifice space to keep the "wow." We trimmed a whole floor off the building—down from six to five—in order to preserve the spectacular character of the space.

The "wow" survived, along with all the places for people to sit, sleep, eat, read, play and collaborate, because we added something else really unique: The Bookbot. I'm sure you've watched the magical Bookbot from the observation window on the first floor (if not, make it a priority on your next trip to Centennial Campus). Someone orders a book at the circulation desk, and its location gets sent to the Bookbot. An automated fork-lift sweeps down the narrow rows of towering drawers (18,000 of them), stops at the precise location, drags out a drawer of books and hauls it back to circulation. The desired book is removed (by a person!), and a book waiting to be stored gets bar-scanned along with its new home, then gets put into the box, and back it goes. Every visitor I take to the library says the same thing: "WOW!"

And they should, because this is revolutionary stuff. Only a couple of other libraries in the world have this kind of storage and retrieval device. No book ever lost, no space wasted, no time wasted. The dense storage uses only about one-ninth the space that would ordinarily be needed, leaving the rest of the room for people—and visualization labs and a soaring entry atrium and a rooftop cafe and Dr. Seuss furniture.

The Hunt Library isn't just—or mostly—about books, but if that is what you're looking for, we"ve still got a traditional quiet room for individual reading and study, with lots of books!

Life is full of compromises, however, and Hunt Library is no exception. Only one company in the world made a Bookbot. And it only came in one size and one shape—an apartment-building-sized rectangle. So, the architects had to design their woven-fabric library around a gigantic concrete box. The grand floating staircase had to go, along with some of the organic shape of the interior spaces.

The future home of the Bookbot was the hole I encountered when I first saw Hunt Library. Our building committee visited the site to see the progress—it was an impressive site, and an impressive sight. Despite a rainy, sloppy day, I was determined to get the full experience and slid down to the bottom of the hole. I felt as if I were actually in the Grand Canyon, a gaping sliver of earth cut out, leading upward, somewhere, to the sunshine.

Eventually the sunshine won, and Hunt Library emerged from the ground to stand tall and proud as the iconic symbol that we envisioned and needed. It keeps winning awards for architecture and for its modern approach to the concept of a library—not just a place to shelve books, but a place for people to access, share and create knowledge. At the time, it was NC State's environmental construction gem, earning a silver certification for energy efficiency, water conservation and sustainable materials.

But what makes me really happy is to walk through and see virtually every one of those bizarre chairs and couches occupied. Doesn't matter whether the people are reading, eating, napping or playing computer games. They are doing it in the James B. Hunt Jr. Library, the library of WOW!

So, there we were, walking down the waterfront in Umeä, Sweden. Umeä is a college town just a bit south of the Arctic Circle, home to the Swedish University of Agricultural Sciences. I was visiting the campus to work on collaborations between their natural resources programs and ours.

After the last meeting, Sharon and I were taking a stroll, enjoying being among the Swedish couples and families enjoying the lovely summer evening. In the distance we saw a dramatic building, with alternating white and dark horizontal features seemingly merging into one another, disguising the actual floor-by-floor structure.

I said, "That looks a lot like Hunt Library."

We walked closer. Sharon said, "It *does* look like Hunt."

As we approached the building, we realized it was—*a library!* What a coincidence, we thought, and we went inside to investigate further. We found a friendly looking librarian (not difficult in Sweden—everyone there looks and is friendly).

We asked, "Can you tell us about the library building?"

She beamed with pride. Yes of course she could tell us about this beautiful new building. "It was designed by the famous Norwegian architecture firm called Snøhetta." This was looking less like a coincidence and more like identity theft.

"The design represents a weaving together of the different purposes inside the building, like a textile gets woven together," she boasted. And, we found out, it was designed and built right after our Hunt Library.

So, Snøhetta, you're busted. Here I am, bragging about how you design each building to the personality of the client, and you've just recycled our design for your next library. Of course, maybe both NC State and Umea, Sweden are really twins separated at birth by tectonic movement.

Either way, it's okay, because imitation is the sincerest form of flattery. And we're proud that in addition to the James B. Hunt Jr. Library, there's now a Swedish branch of the family—the son of WOW!

11

Coach Avent

His teams have lost more games than any other baseball coach in NC State's history. His teams have also *won* more games than any other coach. After 25 years in the dugout, Elliott Avent is, obviously, the longest serving baseball coach in Wolfpack history.

But in a sport that loves statistics, Elliott seems oblivious to the data. When I gave him these figures, he was surprised. But when I told him that he had coached one-third of all the baseball games NC State has ever played, his jaw dropped open. "Wait," he said, "tell me that again." Since NC State started playing baseball in 1903 and through the Covid-shortened 2020 season, the team has played 3824 games. Elliott has been head coach for 1420 of those games, or 37%. And he's won a lot of those games, compiling a 0.626 winning percentage over the whole of his career as our head coach.

Elliott Avent is a classic baseball coach. Short, stocky, excitable, prone to an occasional outburst of colorful language. When we met for an afternoon talk, I was waiting in the reception area of the baseball offices, overlooking Doak Field, named for State's baseball coach during the '20s and '30s. The wall opposite the windows is painted with bigger-than-life action figures of our recent major leaguers—Carlos Rodon, Trea Turner, all 6'-10" of Andrew Brackman stretched out in full windup. Elliott burst through the door, dragging a couple of assistants in his wake, a bit of performance art to animate the mural behind him. He apologized for the wait, paced back and forth, popped in and out of an adjacent door, talking the whole time, as much to himself as others. This, I thought, was just a more nicely decorated dugout for a guy more at home on the base line than in the executive suite.

He's never at a loss for words or opinion, and he's a great storyteller. Yogi Berra without the pinstripes. I remember a tale he told at a dinner at the chancellor's house many years ago. It went something like this:

> I was a farm kid, and we used to raise chickens. My job was to sell the chickens from a little store we had. I had to stay until all the chickens were sold. One evening, we only had one chicken left, and I was eager to sell it and get out of there. A woman from town came in, needing a chicken. When I put it on the scale, she said it was too big and didn't we have a smaller one. I told her yes, and took the chicken into the back room. We didn't have another chicken. I waited a few minutes and came back out, with the same chicken. I put it on the scale, but I used a finger to prop up the scale so the chicken weighed less. That's perfect, she said, and then added, "Since you've been so nice and helpful, I'll buy the first chicken, too."

He claims it's true. I'd like to strap him to a lie-detector.

When the commotion in his office-dugout settled down, we took a walk around the field and I asked Elliott questions—like Jay Bilas does on basketball broadcasts when he walks the length of the court with a player or coach. Bilas' strolls take about a minute. Ours took an hour, a wonderful hour.

"Wooden bats or metal?" I asked, as we strolled from home plate toward first base.

"Wooden, absolutely." Then why does college baseball use metal bats? Follow the money, he said. Metal bats cost about three times as much as wooden bats, but they don't break. The cost of replacing all the broken wooden bats is too high.

"Artificial turf or grass?" I asked.

"Grass, absolutely. I'm a purist. And I hate replays. I love umpires—mostly. They do an incredible job. They are as much a part of the game as the players and coaches. You are safe if the umpire says so, you're out if the umpire says so."

As we stood at second base, he told me about batboys. For a purist, batboys are part of the game, too, and Elliott likes encouraging kids interested in baseball. He usually says yes when a fan asks him if their son or nephew or neighbor could be a batboy for a day. One game, eleven batboys showed up. An assistant told him, "Coach, we don't have any room for the players in the dugout. You gotta get a grip!"

"What do you like best about coaching?" I asked.

His answer surprised me. "I like practice the best." Practice, he said, is where you make an impact on young players. It's where you get to teach them life lessons—all the things we say that college sports is actually about. He likes having the chance to to spend time individually with players, getting to know each of them, helping them develop as players and human beings. I usually had a baseball player or two in my class each semester, and I can vouch for Elliott's results off the field. His players were all conscientious students—came to class, did their work, got pretty decent grades, always had the required permission to miss class for away games. "Don't get me wrong," he said, "I love the games, the competition, gettin' after it. But practice is the real deal. It's where they learn to have the passion of Pete Rose and the mature self-control of Joe DiMaggio."

NC State baseball coach Elliott Avent, with right-handed pitcher Sam Highfill.

Speaking of self-control, I asked, "Why do baseball players chew?"

"For me, it was copying your heroes. I watched them chew tobacco, so I did, too." Since chewing tobacco is a vile habit (my opinion, not his), he later switched to sunflower seeds. "They are so salty, your mouth just puckers up. So for a while, I sucked on Jolly Ranchers. Now I chew bubble gum. I've gotta be the world champion bubble-gum chewer. I work it hard, maybe fifty pieces a game."

But it is the stress in the dugout that creates the need for distraction—whether chewing tobacco or bubble-gum. The measured pace of baseball action causes tension to grow, pitch after pitch, batter after batter, inning after inning. You have to do something to relieve that tension while you are waiting and watching. Elliott mentioned that he sometimes plays with pieces of tape to keep his hands busy. "Once I was talking to Joe Torre, and I asked him how he kept so calm in the dugout. 'Elliott,' he said, 'you have no idea what's swirling around in my stomach.'" (Later, while we talked in Elliott's office, he kept reaching for the tape dispenser, pulling off a piece and beating it to a pulp in his hand.)

"Describe a memorable moment for me," I asked as we rounded third.

Elliott pointed out to left field. "Well, one time was when Brian Adametz made that catch in the outfield to give us the win over Rice that sent us to the College World Series. It was a 17-inning game, and we had a rain delay for a couple of hours. We went in the locker room to wait out the storm. When we started playing again it was after ten o'clock. I expected no one to be in the stands, but when we came on the field, the place was full—maybe there were more people than before the rain. I love our fans. I love NC State."

As we discussed memorable games, I mentioned when Bob Gibson struck out 17 in the 1968 World Series. His eyes lit up, his index finger poked me in the chest, as though I were an umpire needing a talking-to. "That's the day I really got hooked on baseball." He was in sixth grade, and the principal lived in a house across the street from the school. Elliott was sitting in class when the principal came to his classroom to get him. His friends knew he was in for it. But when they left the room, the principal said, "You love baseball, and so do I. We're going over to my house to watch the game. You are never to tell a soul about this." So, Elliott Avent played hooky with the principal as they watched Bob Gibson and the St. Louis Cardinals dismantle the Detroit Tigers. After that, Elliott knew what he wanted to be—a baseball player and coach.

"Tell me something about baseball I don't know" was my final request as we touched home plate.

"Ah," he hesitated, "you know as much about baseball as I do." But then came the dissertation. Baseball, he said, is the best sport. Sure football seems to have taken over television, but watching a baseball game is real entertainment, not just for men, but for everyone. "A baseball game is about having a hot dog, sno-cone and a cold drink; about talking to your kids or friends between innings; about sitting in the sun and enjoying the day." It is truly an engaging sport—sitting close to the players, rooting on your team, relaxing during a pitching change, booing the umpires, getting so tense with runners in scoring position that you need fresh bubble gum.

I couldn't agree more. Talking with Elliott brought back memories of my dad taking me to Wrigley Field to watch the Cubs play on Tuesdays (his day off) during summer vacation in the 1950s. We got there early, for fielding practice, then batting practice. The crowd to watch the pathetic Cubs was always sparse, so we could sit down low for a 90¢ ticket. We always sat down the left field line, in prime position to snag foul balls. An Old Style for him, a Coke for me, and a bag of peanuts in the shell to share. He taught me how to keep score.

He taught me to appreciate hustle and a good play, whichever team made it. Along the way, he taught me a lot about life.

Elliott Avent has taught a lot of kids about life, using the excuse of a baseball game to do it. And for me, that's the best reason for keeping him in the dugout. Let's hope he wins—and loses—many more games for NC State.

12

But is it Art?

Andy Griffith got famous for a little comedy routine he told on Side A of a 45-rpm record in the early 1950s. Before he was Sheriff Taylor from Mayberry, he was a stand-up comic. On the record, he described an event he saw one Saturday afternoon at a North Carolina college. Seems that two bunches of fellas were fightin' over a funny little pumpkin, kickin' it all over a cow pasture painted with white lines, while some convicts in striped shirts ran around blowin' whistles. "What it was," Griffith said, "was football."

Griffith could have made Side B of the record about another mystery that occurs on college campuses, including ours, something called public art. He could try to describe two giant curved discs facing each outside D. H. Hill Library, looking like unfinished ears left over from the carving of Mount Rushmore. Or maybe some statues of wolves, made out of scrap iron—they didn't have enough metal to finish 'em, he might say, but they put 'em up anyhow while they waited for the junk man to make another delivery.

Griffith wouldn't be describing just any art, mind you, but a very specific kind of art: public art. The Association for Public Art, which ought to know, defines public art this way: "Placed in public sites, this art is there for everyone, a form of collective community expression." Beyond that, however, they pretty much punt: "Public art is not an art 'form.' Its size can be huge or small....Its shape can be abstract or realistic (or both), and it may be cast, carved, built, assembled, or painted." Or dug up and piled high, I might add. A public art exhibit when I was at Virginia Tech was a series of sod towers with a sod roof that lasted until the next good rain. Basically, if you can see it without actually trying to see it, that's public art.

According to NC State's 2014 master plan, we have 22 pieces of exterior public art strewn around campus. Four are at the vet school and one at the Arboretum, which leaves 17 actual pieces of art where one of us is likely to encounter it on a stroll across campus.

That's a pretty low total, as universities go. Michael Grenier, a doctoral candidate at the University of Minnesota in 2009, wrote his dissertation about public art on university campuses. Grenier found that big-time schools like NC State average about 40 public art installations. So, we're about half as art-y as our peers, at best. The UNC-Chapel Hill website lists 52 public art installations, but they include several items that are hanging inside building lobbies, no doubt skewing the data in their favor.

The epicenter for public art on our campus is the College of Design, as you might expect. Three of the most artistic pieces are cuddled into the Design neighborhood and a fourth borders it. My favorite is the tangle of contorted red metal stove-pipes entitled "Fit to be Tied." It makes me think of an industrial infinity sign in three dimensions.

I asked NC State's university architect, Lisa Johnson, about our commitment to public art. She smiled—she is usually smiling—and told me, "We need more art, for sure. But we've made some great additions recently." Like what, I asked. She smiled—again—and described *The Swimming Retriever* at the Vet School. The retriever commemorates the contributions of Randall Terry, an ardent dog lover and an equally generous donor to the vet school. "The original idea was for a statue of Mr. Terry and his many golden retrievers, but we learned from people that were close to him that he would have not wanted the art to be about him as he always put his dogs first." Using the university's Art Acquisition Process, which Lisa Johnson initiated to make sure we didn't get any clunkers (no sod columns here, I reckon), we held a global competition. From 37 entries, we chose Vermont sculptor Jim Sardonis.

Campus visitors and dog lovers Suzy and Dale Crawford take a rest with the Swimming Retriever.

Sardonis was inspired by the idea of animals first. Instead of a man surrounded by a pack of adoring dogs, he reversed the scale. His sculpture features the massive head of a retriever—8 times natural size—rising out of the ground as though it is swimming across the landscape. It holds a stick in its mouth, protruding from both sides.

The stick doubles as a bench, inviting us to snuggle up and scratch behind the giant granite ears. The homage to humans is subtle—a tag on the dog's neck sports a bas relief of Mr. Terry. Lisa is right. *Swimming Retriever* is a great addition, a stunning and poignant piece of art, fully capturing the intended theme of the human-animal bond.

But I contend that our commitment to public art on campus shouldn't just be about how many pieces we have, but also their size. If so, then NC State should be competing for the Guinness Book of World Records for public art. Because we have a public art installation that is 200 feet long and 120 feet wide! No, it's not the cow pasture where Andy Griffith watched a fight over a funny little pumpkin.

What it is, is the plaza in front of the Monteith Engineering Research Center on Centennial Campus. The big open space with the crazy brick patterns is there for a more important reason than keeping rain out of the underground parking garage beneath it. It is art! We know it is art for two reasons. One, it has a name. The plaza is known as *Liquid Order*. Two, it was designed by a world-famous artist, Jun Kaneko.

Kaneko hails from Omaha, Nebraska. He works in many media, but mostly in ceramics—so bricks are right up his alley. He likes to make oval discs from clay and decorate them with dots, lines or smaller ovals. Some ovals you can hold in one hand, some can engulf the side of a building. He paints, too, mostly big rectangles filled with straight lines. His work is often the kind that draws long stares and the eternal question, "But is it *art?*"

Kaneko was commissioned to create the artwork in 1995, and it was installed in 1997, for the grand opening of the state-of-the-art engineering research center. And just in time. Kaneko's work was funded under a North Carolina law called the "Art Works in State

Buildings Act." Like similar acts in most states, this law provided that a tiny bit of the appropriation for any state building had to be spent on public art. North Carolina was late coming to this art party, passing its law in 1987, and also a little stingy, since most states devoted 1% to the art cause and North Carolina specified just 0.5%. We also got tired of it in a hurry, too, repealing the law just eight years later, when a budget crisis provided a handy excuse. Kaneko's art piece slipped in at the wire.

Liquid Order can turn you to a pool of liquid sweat if you need to walk across it on a hot summer day.

Liquid Order has lasted, however, and, once you realize it is art, the effect is stunning. Walk across it on a bright July afternoon and you'll be dizzied by the visual spectacle, blinded by the reflection, and fried by the radiating heat. Intricate patterns of parallel lines of white and red bricks zig-zag across the plaza with military precision, then dead-end without warning into a flank of lines advancing from another direction. Kaneko seems to have had some well-organized pattern in mind when he started, but then gave up and started over from another direction, multiple times.

No, he did it on purpose. With a name like *Liquid Order*, something weird has to be going on. Kaneko saw a connection between engineering, science and art. "Engineering," he said "is about finding logic and rules out of apparent chaos. But behind that is creative imagination. Accidents are often the foundation for discoveries in research. It is identical to the way an artist works." So, your research lets you tease a bit of pattern and predictability out of seeming randomness, and you get a little cocky. Then, WHAM, nature says not so fast, little one—I'm changing the rules! Or maybe you can't see anything but chaos in a set of data and, WHAM, nature says stand it on its head, fool—and there is the answer.

Kaneko designed the plaza to be wide open, just as our "inquiring minds" should be, without any other structures interfering with our ability to look and wonder, seek and find. So don't expect a fountain to be built in the middle, or some lovely shade trees to be planted to break up the summer intensity. It is exactly as it was intended. When I walked through recently, an orange caution cone was sitting in the middle of the plaza, and I was irked. Yeah, I suppose a brick might have been out of true and could trip someone, but, darn it, this is art we're messing with here. Have some respect.

And at the end of Side B, I'm sure Andy Griffith would have to agree: "What it was, *was* art!"

———————

Here's a piece of public art on our campus that I'll bet you don't know about—the Fibonacci Spiral. All day long, NC State students walk on, sit on and mostly ignore this peculiar piece of public art. It is built into the plaza between the SAS Building and Park Shops, and it represents a significant mathematical digit—the Golden Ratio. My friend John Briggs, math professor extraordinaire, tried to explain it to me—it is the number 1 plus the square root of 5 divided by 2, or 1.61803398.... The Golden Ratio is a common proportion in nature and a pleasing set of proportions used by architects and other designers.

Because the Golden Ratio can be represented visually, let's conquer it that way, as the designers of the SAS Building did. A close approximation of the Golden Ratio occurs in the shape of another piece of mathematical trivia, the Fibonacci Spiral, named after a Pisan mathematician (who got it from India). Imagine a chambered nautilus cut in half and you've more or less got the idea.

Starting near the center of the SAS Building plaza, our representation of the Golden Ratio is a big curving Fibonacci Spiral that takes a few laps around what we call Stinson Plaza. It wraps clockwise around the area, first on the ground, then briefly as a sitting wall before hitting the ground again. As the spiral spreads out, it dives into the building itself, in the form of a long curve of floor tiles along a hallway. It escapes the building, heads across the street and becomes a long curved sitting wall in front of Park Shops, usually covered up by eating, reading, talking, napping students with no idea they are participating in a real-life geometry proof. It crosses back over the street and then punctures the SAS Building again, dead-ending ingloriously into a lonely corner.

I wonder, if you sat at the very center wearing an aluminum foil hat, might the ghost of Isaac Newton give you some help on calculus homework?

13

A Train Track Runs Through It

A Boy Scout is always prepared. Apparently, a university's executive officers must be prepared, too. When I was provost, it seemed like we were regularly involved in simulating some impending disaster or other. What if hurricane rains flooded the computer building? What if the Bird Flu actually flew to North Carolina? What if the Vet School's cows staged a sit-in on Hillsborough Street?

The most likely unexpected disaster we had to fear, however, was the possible derailment of a train carrying toxic substances. You see—as we all know—a train track runs through our campus. One end to the other, it bisects campus like the spinal column on a long, thin fish, ribs of roads and tunnels heading off to the north and south. The track carries passenger trains en-route from Washington to Charlotte and the reverse—those aren't a problem. But it also carries freight trains, usually loaded with coal, but maybe, sometimes, with toxic chemicals.

So, one day the executive officers simulated how we would handle a derailment and spill of dangerous chemicals. Our mock emergency response occupied a morning usually reserved for administrative meetings. At least this was going to be better than the usual committee reports! Several of us huddled in the chancellor's conference room—our control center—checking in with our health and safety staffs, issuing shelter-in-place warnings to the campus community, handling calls from concerned parents and trying to be sure that everyone knew this was "a test, only a test." Finally, we cleared the debris, declared victory and went to a celebratory lunch—as far from the train tracks as we could get.

The university's founders would be amazed by our simulation because they never intended the university to breach the railroad tracks. As the Facilities Division website states, "Few if any of NC state's founders foresaw the growth that the university has experienced." But we did need *someplace* to call home. North Carolina College of Agriculture and Mechanic Arts, our original moniker, was born in 1887, and we immediately set to work on Holladay Hall, the first campus building, opened in 1889. At the time, Holladay handled everything—classrooms, offices, gym, dormitory, cafeteria, everything. The Mechanical Building followed a year later, and a dairy barn was built next, behind Holladay (never forget we started as "agriculture and mechanic arts").

Next, several small dormitories joined the campus. Then we got busy, moving westward with a series of buildings that eventually enclosed what we now call the Court of Carolina. By 1920, when we started calling ourselves North Carolina State College, the neighborhood was starting to feel crowded.

But that dang railroad was in the way. It had squatter's rights, having sliced through the landscape much earlier than the campus. The tracks that the NC State family crosses under or over every day were laid down starting in 1836, allowing the Raleigh & Gaston Railroad to begin operation on its amazing 86-mile route—not surprisingly, from Raleigh to Gastonia—in April, 1840. Unfortunately, the line wasn't profitable. The private company that owned it punted, and the state government took over its operations. Profitable or not, the train track wasn't going anywhere. And if NC State was going to grow, it had to grow around them.

Both freight and passenger trains rumble over our heads every day, as we pass through tunnels from one side of campus to the other.

Agricultural fields had always been south of the tracks, but the first structures—dairy barns to replace the one behind Holladay—were built there in 1909. After World War I, though, the university was growing and it just needed more space. A high priority was a gym, because physical education classes were replacing the mandatory military training that had ended with armistice. The first real "campus" building on the other side of the tracks, therefore, was Thompson Gymnasium, opened in 1925. It was state of the art, with a basketball arena where the Wolfpack played, a second gym, indoor pool and elevated indoor running track (When Reynolds Coliseum was built after the next world war, Thompson was turned over to other uses, including the performance theaters and the craft shops that still operate there).

I once saw a drawing of an early plan for how the university might expand beyond the railroad tracks. The plan called for a broad open space, perhaps a quarter-mile wide, that covered the tracks, running from Patterson Hall all the way to where Reynolds Coliseum now sits. It would have been the main "quad" for the university, unifying the two parts of campus that are now officially called North Campus and Central Campus. No one can tell me why that plan wasn't implemented, but I'll bet the legislature thought it was too expensive.

Instead, we settled for a "Freshman Quadrangle." In 1925, along with Thompson, a new dormitory—Bagwell Hall—sprouted along Pullen Road. Nothing new was added until 1939, when Becton and Berry Dormitories joined Bagwell to surround the green rectangle now completed by the Quad Commons. Clark Hall—also a dormitory when built—rounded out the complex. These four dormitories were built using Public Works Administration funding, one of the programs of President Franklin Roosevelt's New Deal to pull the country out of the Great Depression.

Since then, it has been campus sprawl on steroids, south of the tracks and everywhere else. A quick count on the campus map shows about 50 buildings north of the railroad tracks and 65 between the tracks and Western Boulevard. But that's just part of the story. The university's website of facilities inventory shows that we have 1,122 buildings! Since the university is 133 years old, that means we've averaged adding a bit more than 8 buildings every year of our existence.

Not all of those buildings are massive, of course. Like the eight "CALS Feed Shelters" in Bahama. That's Bahama, North Carolina, in northern Durham County, not the less famous place in the

Caribbean. But some are massive, like the James B. Hunt Jr. Library. At 258,800 square feet, it is our largest building. As the Facilities Division brags, a football field could fit inside it.

Our biggest area of growth, of course, has been Centennial Campus. The state government allocated just over 800 acres of the former state mental hospital to NC State in the mid 1980s. We opened our first building on the campus in 1989, and the entire College of Textiles moved to Centennial in 1991. A quick count of building on Centennial is, well, it isn't that easy. We have university buildings, private buildings, collaborative buildings, leased buildings, other government buildings—all squatting there to create a "community built around knowledge." But, the total is pretty close to 50 buildings, about the same number as on the North Campus, where it all started.

I actually like the idea that the railroad comes through campus. It is a great metaphor for the university's role in society. Sure, we exist in our own right to discover knowledge and to learn and teach. But as a Land-Grant University, with missions of teaching, research and extension, we also are connected to the rest of society, just as a railroad connects the people of one place to the people of another place. Their ideas, vision and aspirations travel with them, just as ours should extend far beyond campus to make the world a better place.

So, next time a train rumbles over your head as you walk through a tunnel, think about the experience as a metaphor for life. And imagine where you and your ideas might just take you—and the world.

14

Bob Patterson

I don't recall exactly when Bob Patterson entered my NC State life. Seems like he's always been there. We have a lot in common. We're both old, both got our doctorates from Cornell, both focused more on teaching than research in our later years and, most importantly, both care deeply about students and sustainability. He teaches his main class—STS 323, World Population and Food Prospects—in 2215 Williams, the auditorium across from his office, where I also taught conservation for several years. I've probably talked more with him over the years about important things than I have with all the faculty in my department combined.

But I'm not writing about Bob because he is like an older brother. I'm writing because I know what thousands of students also know—that Bob Patterson is an institution all his own, an institution as valuable as the corn and soybean crops he has nurtured. He's been a faculty member here for more than half a century—he became an assistant professor in 1968—teaching his heart out for longer than most of his faculty colleagues have been alive. A website about NC State without a chapter about Bob Patterson would be like *Casablanca* without Ilsa or *Star Wars* without Han Solo.

Bob is a professor in the Department of Crop and Soil Sciences. He's worked on lots of crops all over the world. He is a true global thinker. At our recent lunch, I gave him a copy of my book, *Nature's Allies*. It features a biography of Wangari Maathai, the Kenyan woman who won the Nobel Peace Prize for planting 50 million trees. He then told me about a time in the early 1980s when he was visiting Nairobi on a research project. He had learned about a Scottish agronomist who was doing work near there. Driven by his insatiable curiosity, he arranged to visit the scientist's lab and field location to see his research. On the hour-long ride to the site, his taxi took him past groves of newly planted trees, with signs identifying them as Greenbelt Movement plantations. He asked his driver, who told him about Wangari Maathai. Since then, she has been one of his heroes. Mention just about anything, about anywhere, and Bob's face will light up to either tell you about his related experience or ask you more, much more, about your own.

Our relationship began in earnest when we taught study abroad at the Prague Institute, now re-christened as the "NC State Gateway to Europe." Bob was a regular there; I was a novice. In the summer of 2012, we stayed at the same hotel, so we generally started our days together over breakfast. He always—and I mean always—came into the breakfast room with something to share. He'd read an article about forestry and wanted to discuss it. He'd seen a strange fish at a market, took a photo and wanted me to identify it. He was planning a field trip and wanted my advice on how to make it more meaningful for the students (as if he needed my advice).

His field trips were famous, perhaps infamous. He and his students spent several days working at an organic farm out in the countryside. They slept in primitive cabins, got up early, ate down-home Czech food. They worked—planted, hoed, harvested—alongside the resident farmers, suffering the heat, rain and bugs just as the farmers did. "Think and Do the Extraordinary" is our current campus slogan, something Bob and his students lived for years. They came back caked in mud, exhausted—and radiant. Study abroad is transformative, we know; study abroad with Bob Patterson is extraordinarily transformative.

Bob Patterson in his Williams Hall office.

Bob told me about the origin of his principal course, World Population and Food Prospects. Just after Bob joined the NC State faculty, legendary Chancellor John Caldwell got together a group to discuss adding cross-disciplinary courses that both students and faculty members had been demanding. It was the late 1960s, and students were demanding all sorts of things, including interesting courses. But the time was also the height of the Cold War and the emergence of the environmental movement. The committee agreed on three courses as priorities—Nuclear Proliferation, Humans and the Environment, and World Population and Food Prospects. Bob, his colleagues said, you're the agronomist, so you teach about food. He first taught the course in 1970, with three other faculty. Soon, however, the other teachers' department heads made waves about them teaching a non-major course, and they all backed out. Bob took it over himself in 1974 and has taught it ever since, every semester, first to about 60 students per year, now to about 200 students per semester.

Bob is not a modern faculty member. Modern faculty members tend to have sleek, tidy offices with minimalist furnishings that look like interior-decorating photo shoots. Not Bob. His office is packed—lined floor to ceiling with shelves bulging with real books; the desk and work table are covered in stacks of journals and newspaper articles; the walls are papered with overlapping layers of photos, sayings and hand-drawn pictures; the door is covered in notices of upcoming (and often long past) events. Seed pods, stalks of leaves and soil samples mix with souvenirs of international research and teaching on random surfaces. Plants grow in front of the windows. Drop in and he'll say, "Ah, I've got something here I was wanting to ask you about…" and pull an article off one of the stacks to share. "If you have time, please read this and tell me what you think." Most of us these days regard paper as our enemy, but to Bob it is an old friend. Walk into 2212 Williams Hall and you know you're in a faculty office, not a hip corporate think-tank.

His office is like Grand Central Station. A student worker is usually posted in the outer room, prepping his handouts for class and fending off random visitors (like me). It doesn't help. Everyone has business with Bob. Advisees need advice, Park Scholars need mentoring, club leaders need the upcoming program confirmed, staff and junior faculty need signatures and some wisdom, former students need hugs.

To Bob Patterson, "professor" isn't a job, it's a mission. "My parents wanted me to do something no one in the family had done—get a college education," he told me. "I came down to State as a student, scared to death." But he got over the fear and kept at it, and he hurried right back here after completing his doctorate at Cornell. Since then, he's won about every teaching award the university, the UNC system and the agriculture profession have to offer. He was designated an Alumni Distinguished Undergraduate Professor in 1981; although no good records exist, the Provost's Office assured me that he is undoubtedly the oldest ADUP still working—and still eager to inspire the next class of students.

Inspiring is not a compliment I use lightly or often, but Bob earns it. Once I asked him to speak to a group of doctoral students from Brazil, England and NC State whom I was hosting for a nine-day seminar on climate change. Of course he said yes. He talked about the need to preserve the biodiversity of old cultivars of plants—heritage crops, they are called—that might be more adaptable to the hotter, drier climate that is coming. He described the international seed bank that the United Nations had established in Aleppo, Syria. Then he talked about how wars and unrest in the Middle East had destroyed that city—and the seed bank. Most of us were crying, including Bob, for the damaged lives of those people and the damaged sustainability of our earth.

No, Bob Patterson is not a modern faculty member. He doesn't flip the classroom, avoids powerpoints with background music and embedded video and has trouble sticking to the syllabus. What he has is fifty-plus years of deep and broad knowledge about people and the world. What he has is sincerity and caring that transcends all the new-fangled ideas of pedagogy.

Many times I talked with students who were taking both his course and mine. Invariably they would explain, without knowing it, what separates Bob Patterson from the rest of us: "I really like your course," they would say, "but I *love* Dr. Patterson."

15

Counting Plates

Leonard and Penny start up their relationship again on a particular episode of *The Big Bang Theory*. They go out on a "second first date." When Penny flirtingly tells Leonard that he sounds like a nerd, Leonard replies, "Not just a nerd—the King of Nerds!"

Naw, he's not the king—I am. I know the lyrics to most Broadway musicals, wear long white socks with shorts and put ketchup on, well, everything. But here's the clincher: I count plates. License plates. From different states. Nerd to the 50th power.

Sharon and I take lots of road trips, and keeping track of how many different state license plates we see makes the time go a little faster. We keep a Melissa and Doug puzzle of the United States in the car; each state has a little token that you turn to keep track of your progress. If you don't get at least 40 states during a summer week at North Myrtle Beach, you just aren't trying.

I often count license plates on my walks around campus. I can't help it. For several years, a car usually parked in an RA spot near Sullivan Hall sported a North Dakota plate. The Reynolds Coliseum lot had a big-butt pick-up from South Dakota. Someone from Nebraska parked next to the softball field. For a semester the lots around Wolf Village were good for a Utah and a Maine.

So, one day when pouring rain threatened my campus walk, I retreated to the Dan Allen parking deck to assess our license-plate diversity at NC State. I walked every aisle on every floor. My haul was pretty rich—32 different states were parked in the deck. All the eastern states were present, of course, including the Holy Grail of the Atlantic Coast: Rhode Island. Most of the Midwestern states showed up as well, along with all the West Coast and several interior states—Colorado, Kansas, New Mexico, Arizona, and Arkansas.

That got me wondering about the student population at NC State. Who are we? Where do we come from? To find out, I had lunch with long-time campus experts, Tommy Griffin, recently retired as Director of Admissions, and Louis Hunt, Senior Vice Provost for Enrollment Management and Services. Both of these fellows have worked here so long they remember when students submitted applications on paper—through the mail!

Turns out that, theoretically, I could have found all fifty states on the rear of cars parked on campus. NC State enrolls undergraduate students from every state. We don't necessarily admit students from all states every year, occasionally missing Montana or Wyoming. But with four or five or six cohorts on campus at all times, we blanket the nation.

Most out-of-state students hale from our neighbors, Virginia and South Carolina. Other states up and down the eastern seaboard fill out most of the rest of the top ten. But two spots in the top ten are a fer piece—California and Texas. Californians, it seems, can come to NC State, pay out-of-state tuition here, fly home for holidays and still save money over in-state tuition there.

Back in 1986, UNC President Bill Friday started looking at the enrollment statistics, worrying that the university might be getting overrun with out-of-state students. He recommended that the Board of Governors adopt an 18% limit on non-North-Carolina students, and they did. Neither Tommy or Louis knew why the limit was 18%, and Bill Friday, bless his soul, now lives in the big university in the sky and can't share his logic. But his limit has stuck for more than 30 years. NC State enrolls just north of 16% outsiders, with little danger that we'll go much higher. UNC-Chapel Hill always flirts with the limit, sometimes going over slightly and giving back some funds to the state treasury as a penalty. Someday I'm going to sneak over there, disguised in baby blue, and count license plates.

We get a pretty healthy dose of international students as well. Four percent of our incoming students each year come from other countries. China and India lead the way, just as you'd expect from the two countries with the largest human populations on earth. They also love our heavy emphasis on engineering and science. But we enroll students from more than 120 countries—about half of the countries in the world. Wish they brought cars with them. A Bangladesh license plate in North Carolina would make be Master of the Nerd-iverse!

I asked Tommy and Louis what's different today about admitting students than 15 years or so ago, when they were relative rookies. "Everything is different," said Tommy, "and everything is pretty much the same." The process is what's different. Like all parts of life, the admissions process is more and more automated. Students apply on-line with a common application that is accepted by the majority of colleges and universities across the country. Because submitting applications has become so easy, students are applying to many more schools than in the past—about 7 is the average now. Louis recalled one student who applied to 17 schools! Just click the button and pay the fee. Our end of the process is automated as well—when it is time to send out the acceptance letters, we click the button and an email goes to each accepted student, hopefully a Wolfpacker-in-waiting rather than someone using us as their safety school.

You can learn a lot by reading license plates.

What isn't automated—and what remains the same—is the individual care that's given to each application as it arrives. Admissions officers still read every application. They might even pay more attention than in the past, because the admissions process is now "holistic," considering a wider array of factors than in the past. My wife was an admissions officer at Virginia Tech in the late 1980s and during the winter months, she'd trudge home every evening with a box of application files to review after supper as I put the kids to bed. Same thing now, said Tommy, except the applications live in the cloud and follow you around everywhere.

But figuring out in advance who will succeed and who won't is still hard. When I asked if universities had learned much over the years about what factors—grades, class rank, test scores, co-curricular activities, essays, recommendations—are most predictive,

Tommy and Louis both shrugged. The intangibles still matter a lot: how students will react to being away from home, whether motivation will kick in or fade away, if bad habits will grow into fatal flaws or be replaced by good habits. Answers to those questions don't show up in the applications. So the admission decision often still rests with the gut feeling of the reviewer.

Thankfully, listening to your gut is generally a good idea. Saying "yes" to a prospective student turns out to be the right answer most of the time. Student retention rates at NC State keep going up, along with graduation rates. In my 17 years here, our six-year graduation rate rose from under 70% to over 80%, a pretty phenomenal increase.

As we were ending our lunch at the outdoor café, I asked Tommy and Louis what the future looked like. "Rosy," they both answered. Just then, diners celebrating some happy event at the adjacent table turned on a bubble machine. Soon, we were engulfed in a magical cloud of bubbles. "See," Louis said, "Rosy!"

I'll buy that. And on my walk back to the office, I passed a car with a NC license plate that read, "LUVSTATE." License-plate nerds are never wrong!

16

TGIF

Sculpture is rare on the NC State campus—remember the story about public art? Particularly rare is sculpture that depicts actual people rather than wolves. Many university campuses are peppered with statues designed for inspiration—former presidents, famous alumni, world leaders. Apart from the four statues of basketball personalities that now greet you at the renovated Reynolds Coliseum—Kay Yow, Norm Sloan, Jim Valvano and Everett Case—only two statues of real people grace the NC State campus.

One is the *Strolling Professor*, in the Gardner Arboretum between Burlington and Patterson Halls. The *Strolling Professor* is a life-sized statue that portrays Dr. William R. Johnson, Professor of Chemistry. For 25 years, Johnson taught introductory chemistry classes, becoming a beloved part of our STEM heritage. He was also well known to walk around campus, engrossed in whatever chemistry book he was reading. The statue was erected in 1986; since then, it has become good luck to rub his brass head before taking a chemistry test.

The other is smaller and less noticeable—a bust in the Governor Scott Courtyard between Kilgore and Fox Halls. The bust is of William Friday—Bill Friday as he was known for three-fourths of a century in North Carolina. Whether you rub his head or not, having

Bill Friday on our campus has been great luck. "Thank God it's Friday" means a lot more than the excitement for the weekend ahead.

Bust of Bill Friday on the NC State campus.

Bill Friday served as the President of the University of North Carolina system for thirty years, from 1956 to 1986. He retired then at the age of 65, a victim of a rule he himself helped establish early in his tenure, making retirement mandatory at that age. I suspect he never thought he'd remain president for that long.

Truth is, he never intended to work in higher education at all. Friday started college at Wake Forest University, but saw the light and transferred to NC State after one year. He was destined to follow his father into the textile industry, so he became a textile major, graduating in 1941. He never particularly loved book-learning; as his biographer, William Link, wrote, "Performance in the classroom had never been among Friday's strengths."[1] What he loved were sports and student government—and eventually a young lady named Ida Howell. He served as a "spotter" for the announcers at Wolfpack football games, later started reporting on games, and ended as the sports editor for *The Technician*. His sports reporting made him well-known around campus, leading to his election as president of the student body. His interest in Ida continued to grow, blossoming into a lifetime of what Link "described as a 'wonderful marriage' that grew into a strong partnership."[2]

With World War II on the horizon, Friday sought a commission in the Navy. While he waited, he took a temporary job at NC State—the only job he'd ever have here—as the chief dormitory assistant in student affairs. Within a few months, his commission came through and he spent the next four years as a naval supply officer. On his discharge in 1946, he attended law school at Chapel Hill. Once again, outside his plans and against his better judgment, he took a university job, this time as assistant dean of students at UNC.

When an administrative combination of UNC, NC State and UNC-Greensboro occurred in 1951, Friday moved to the "Consolidation Office" as assistant to the university president. A few years later, when that president moved on to a federal government post, a national search concluded that they had the right guy already in the building. In 1956, at the age of 35, Bill Friday became the president of the University of North Carolina.

Bill Friday was a special kind of leader. He never sought the center of attention, was never boisterous, never confrontational. He treated everyone with equal respect, whether a janitor or a chancellor. Link describes him as a quiet motivator who worked often within the shadows. Long after his retirement as president, I occasionally saw him on a Saturday morning at the Raleigh Farmers' Market. We'd talk for a few minutes about campus; he was always interested and supportive, but he never lectured or criticized. When I think about Bill Friday, however, I'm reminded of a description I've read of another leader—don't be fooled by his apparent softness; it is only the moss growing on a granite-like foundation.

Friday put his granite foundation to good use as president of UNC. To be sure, he wasn't the perfect candidate for the job. He admitted that as a student he "really didn't do much academic work."[3] He had never taught a course, had no scholarly credentials and his experience was minimal. In fact, when he was offered the job by the Board of Trustees, their condition was that he agree to work with a seasoned academic administrator that they had chosen to be his coach. Friday stomped on that idea—the first of many times his granite showed—but the trustees appointed him anyway.

And "Thank God it's Friday"—because we needed him. His issues began on a familiar battleground—the basketball court. North Carolina had established an annual basketball tournament called the Dixie Classic. The four big-time North Carolina schools—State, UNC, Duke and Wake Forest—played the tournament against four invited national powers. The Dixie Classic was the template for what we now call the Final Four. But in 1961, it was the finale for the tournament, when officials learned gamblers had bribed players to manipulate the point-spread for the games. Friday's commitment to the integrity of our universities made his decision easy, if not popular: The Dixie Classic was finished—and it has never been played again.

His first decade as president was a time of protest on university campuses, including in North Carolina. In 1963, in the midst of the Cold War and as civil unrest on universities campuses was turning ugly, the North Carolina legislature passed a law that restricted who could and could not speak on university campuses—the so-called "Speaker Ban." From the beginning and for the next five years, Friday railed against the law. A university, he asserted, could only be useful or effective if it were free of political control. Eventually, a federal court ruled that Friday was correct and the legislature wrong.

Among all the great qualities that I admired in Bill Friday, that was the greatest—he cared most about the integrity of the university. Once, when as provost I had to make a personnel decision that I thought he would dislike, I called him to explain the situation before it became public. He said, "Larry, you don't need to worry about me. Your job is to do what's best for NC State."

Bill Friday understood what the university was about, and he wasn't afraid to say so. Consequently, he achieved the highest regard as an academic leader, before and well after his retirement as president of UNC in 1986. He advised Presidents Johnson and Carter, chaired major scholarly commissions, helped implement the vision for the Research Triangle Park, and led the creation of the then 16-campus University of North Carolina system. In the early 1990s, he returned to his interest in athletics, co-chairing the Knight Commission. The title of the commission's report says it all: *Keeping Faith with the Student-Athlete*. Bill Friday always kept faith with the purpose of a university—wherever it took him.

When I was provost, I had lots of ideas for change, some good, some not. Consequently, I riled some folks, both inside and outside the university, on occasion. So, I loved when Bill Friday made a promotional videotape for NC State as part of a development project we were beginning. He said a lot of laudatory things about our campus, but one phrase stuck out. He said, "If your university isn't making you uncomfortable every so often, it's not doing its job."

We put up the bust of Bill Friday in the summer of 2008 (and UNC-Chapel Hill has one just like it). It fades into the background a bit now, especially as the surrounding shrubbery has grown around it. Few, I suspect, have stopped to look or read the accompanying plaque. Hundreds of students, faculty and staff walk by it every day. Fewer still understand what his leadership has meant to our campus, our university and our state.

But now you do. And next time you think, "TGIF," remember that it is really Bill Friday, not happy hour, that you're thankful for.

17

What the Other Hand Does

Many years ago, I was diagnosed with tendonitis in my right elbow. I'd like to claim tennis elbow, but the closest my elbow ever got to tennis was holding the potato chip bowl as I munched my way through Wimbledon. The doctor decided I should wear a sling for six weeks.

Whew, I thought, that's lucky—I'm left-handed and the sling will be on my right arm. Shouldn't be a problem at all, just inconvenient enough to get some sympathy and a pass on mowing the lawn.

I was wrong. Way wrong. That other hand is about as important as college basketball in the Triangle. That other hand holds the fork when you're cutting your steak. It changes the radio station while you're driving. It makes putting on your socks possible.

Where is he going with this, that's what you're wondering. But stay with me, because I'm about to make a very important point. Maybe the most important point in this whole left-handed book.

When I walk around campus, I try to notice what's going on around me. Students are streaming in and out of Clark Dining Hall. Grounds members are mowing grass, raking leaves, or shoveling snow. Mechanics are dropping down manholes to tinker with the steam system. Maintenance folks are emptying trash containers. Nurses are taking a walk at lunch.

This fellow is as much a part of achieving the university's mission as a professor in her classroom or a coach on the sidelines.

All that activity makes me think, who does the work of the university? Most people would name faculty members first; cynical people might put graduate students at the top of the list And, yes, those two groups do play a major role in driving the university bus down the road.

But academic folks are only one hand of the pair that makes the wheels go around. The other hand, the one we don't pay attention to unless it's in a sling, is just as important. And that other hand is the set of crucial folks that we lump into an anonymous category of "staff." Staff means everyone else at the university who isn't a faculty member.

That anonymous crowd generally gets treated like, well, they get treated poorly. They don't get teaching awards or promotion bonuses or time off to do consulting. They don't get merit pay or the chance to work at home when it suits them. And outsiders think we have too many of them around. University leaders always get grief from faculty members and legislators that they are hiring too many staff and not enough faculty. And whenever the budget-cut ax starts flying, it whacks away at staff first, the ones who don't have tenure.

I'm here to set the record straight. We de-value staff at our own peril—students and faculty members alike. In a recent book on university administration, a grateful provost (me) wrote about the role of "staff" in making the university function:

> Ask a faculty member how a student actually graduates—how the grades and credit hours get captured and saved, how a student's accomplishments get recorded and compared with the requirements, how those records turn into a diploma and transcript. Ask them about tutoring—how tutors get selected and trained, how we know which students need what help, how it gets scheduled, how we monitor to make sure nothing shady is going on, how we pay for it, how we monitor and assess success. Odds are, they won't have a clue.
>
> As I'm revising this chapter, I have just finished giving a final exam, grading it, and posting the final semester grades. In so doing, I called on the assistance of instructional technology, copy center, disability services, registration and records, computer services, departmental assistants, academic advising, janitorial services, and, no doubt, several other offices that are entirely invisible to me. Bless their hearts.

And that's just the story about giving grades and some other academic tomfoolery. What about the work that goes on just to keep the lights on? And the leaves raked? And the buses running?

Study after study show that students decide where to enroll for all sorts of reasons that have nothing to do with the quality of the faculty. They are influenced by how much they like the campus tour, usually led by admissions "staff" or student interns. They form an impression of the university based on the landscaping—the groundkeeping "staff" who keep the place in bloom and tidy are truly important. They eat a meal or two in the dining halls, judging whether the "staff" are satisfactory cooks. And they all want to check out the gym and student center, both run by "staff," not faculty.

I could keep rattling on for pages—about financial aid, recycling, study abroad, the health center—but the point should be clear. Just as Napoleon said that "an army marches on its stomach," so does a university march on the feet of its "staff." They perform thousands of tasks needed to allow the small city we call NC State to operate and a group of very well treated faculty members to teach, do research and create.

And, lest anyone think we are staff-rich at NC State, let me stop you right there. A recent study showed that the national average ratio of staff to faculty is 3.79:1. At State we have, according to official data, 2336 faculty and 6314 staff. That's a ratio of 2.70:1. To get up to the national average, we'd have to hire another 2500 people into staff positions. Of course we're not going to do that, but do you know what that means? Our colleagues without advanced degrees are working really hard on our behalf.

My advice is this, to both students, faculty, and even alumni coming back for a visit: First, try putting your socks on with one hand tomorrow—that'll remind you that you need two hands. Second, next time you cross paths with a person shoveling snow or emptying the trash or painting a wall, don't just walk by with your head down and your air-pods drowning out the world around you. Instead, look up, smile and say hello—and thanks.

18

It's Written in the Bricks

Now that Professor Robert Langdon has deciphered all the clues in *The DaVinci Code* and saved the world, perhaps we could give him a real challenge. Maybe we can get him to decipher the enbricked codes on the NC State campus.

I sometimes imagine what a future Indiana Jones might think when she digs up our campus a millennium or two into the future. Bricks are everywhere, so they must have been the cheapest form of paving available. But, wait, every so often strange patterns appear. The biggest area—no doubt destined to be the Stonehenge for future archeologists—is an expanse with zig-zag lines running in all directions and a huge S in the middle. Is it a map? Are they religious symbols? Are they mazes describing the changing majors of college students?

Some symbols are fairly easy to figure out. "$E=mc^2$" near the Free Expression Tunnel pretty well describes our faculty and students. The porch in front of Leazer Hall mirrors the pattern of the front of the building—a nice metaphor for design students.

And then there are the Greek letters running up the sidewalks of Dan Allen and adjacent to Reynolds Coliseum. Shelly Brown Dobek, Director of Fraternity and Sorority Life, explained that the symbols along Dan Allen represent organizations that belong to

the Panhellenic and Interfraternity Council, the 31 social fraternities and sororities on campus (plus or minus, of course, depending
which ones are suspended at any particular time). According to
Shelly, the symbols are arranged in order of each organization's ap-
pearance on campus. Sigma Nu is oldest, at the top of the hill adjacent to Biltmore Hall and running down to the bottom. Then the
string starts again at the top of the hill on the West side of the street,
down to whatever is the youngest. The symbols get renewed regularly, she says, at considerable cost to her department.

What will future archeologists think about our brand of petroglyphs?

The Greek symbols near Reynolds Coliseum represent groups in
the National Pan-Hellenic Council (NPHC), traditionally African
American fraternities and sororities. Toni Thorpe, an NC State tradition herself and recently retired from the African American Cul-

tural Center, told me that the placing of these symbols has special meaning. They replicate a tradition at Historically Black Colleges and Universities, at which a central campus area is laid out with specific "plots" for each of the student organizations. The plots have a plaque or some other way of identifying the group, are sometimes painted with the group's colors and may have a bench where members can gather. In the 1990s, symbols for our NPHC groups were placed in the sidewalk. As the number of groups expanded—now numbering nine—there wasn't enough space or money to redo the plots. Eventually, the hope is, an expanded sidewalk in front of Reynolds will be able to house symbols for all the groups.

But others are more confusing. Why is Patterson Hall surrounded by a series of three parallel stripes in the sidewalks? Why do diamond shapes appear at seemingly random sites around campus? And why do chevrons show up on the sidewalk across from Derr Track?

And how about the three Greek letters in front of the Music Building? Now that's an interesting story. They represent Mu Beta Psi, a music honorary for non-music majors. MBP was started on our campus in 1925, and now six active chapters and an alumni group. The brick designs were installed in the 1990s, according to MBP alum Logan Graham, formerly Coordinator of Music for the Music Department. The letters were installed at the same time that two pointed brick arches were installed between Price Hall and the old Talley Student Center. They were affectionately called "Percy's Peaks," after Percy Price, the first director of music at NC State, from 1924 to his death in 1933. Price founded MBP—and the orchestra, men's glee club, marching band and a drum and bugle corps. The peaks are gone now, with the renovation of Talley, but MBP is still around, and so are their bricks.

The Greek letters near Reynolds Coliseum symbolize our
African American sororities and fraternities.

Farther along the sidewalk, in front of Burlington and Alexander
residence halls, are the weirdest set of markings. In a repeated set of

bricks, a pattern gradually emerges, starting with a few yellow bricks to which others are added in the next set, and so on. A member of the grounds crew once told me the pattern was a mathematical game that had been dreamed up by an early faculty member, but the basis for the pattern was lost in history. We'll leave that to future sleuths.

The most interesting artifact for future archeologists, however, will be the Block S shapes distributed around campus. There are a lot of them. I've recorded about a score, including ones that are painted on, like in the intersection of Dan Allen and Dunn. But they aren't everywhere, so the places marked with a Block S must be pretty special. That makes sense for the three Block S patterns that surround Reynolds Coliseum—but what about the one at the entrance to the Sullivan Drive parking deck? (well, maybe future archeologists will figure out how important parking was.)

In the Brickyard, close to the new plaza where Harrelson Hall used to be, is a small yellow brick rectangle. About four bricks by two bricks in size. In that carefully constructed maze of the Brickyard, why would there be a little yellow rectangle? Just one insignificant little rectangle walked across by hundreds of Wolfpackers every day without even noticing it. I suspect I'm the only person around who knows why it is there.

So, here's the rest of the story. When NC State began to think seriously about campus sustainability and I was dean of Natural Resources, I formed and chaired the Campus Environmental Sustainability Team (it's now called the Sustainability Council). As part of our efforts, we established the Green Brick Awards to acknowledge the efforts of members of our campus to promote sustainability; one student, staff member and faculty member are chosen annually for the awards (I have one myself!). For the first award ceremony, we had that yellow rectangle embedded in the Brickyard. Inside the yellow border, we placed commemorative bricks about sustainability and winners of the awards. That night, the engraved bricks were stolen. The commemorative bricks were immediately replaced by plain red bricks, and the commemorative idea brick idea has gone away. But the little yellow rectangle remains, a mystery written in the bricks.

19

Operation Gwamba

For reasons I'll not explain, I was looking into what happened in conservation on February 1. Any year, but on that particular date. A rifle through several on-this-day websites revealed little of note, except one mention that the Afobaka Dam in Suriname was closed on February 1, 1964.

Let me save you from googling Suriname, because I did it for you. Suriname is the smallest country in South America, sitting bravely on its northeast coast, backed by Brazil and nestled between Guyana and French Guiana (two other countries I have to look up whenever they are mentioned). It was a Dutch colony until becoming independent in 1975.

With a little more noodling around the web, the story got more interesting. I discovered that when the lake behind Afobaka Dam was filling with water, a massive rescue of trapped wildlife was conducted. Called Operation Gwamba, the effort saved more than 10,000 animals from drowning. The total included over 2000 three-fingered sloths, 167 snakes (including deadly poisonous bushmasters), a bunch of other creatures and 1 house cat (their record-keeping is impressive). All of this is documented in a little book called *Time is Short and the Water Rises*.

On a whim, I entered the title into our library website, expecting nothing. But there it was—in D. H. Hill Library—QL 246 .W34 1967.

There it was, and the library, bless its heart, let me borrow it. A lonely little paperback, not rebound in typical library style, but clothed sadly in its torn and decomposing paper cover. It cost 95cents when new. The book still had a piece of paper glued inside the front cover to record due dates when someone checked it out. There were no due dates stamped in it. I suspect that no one had ever checked this book out of our library before I did.

There it had been for half a century, hiding in the stacks, waiting patiently for someone, anyone, to want to read it. I'm happy for the lonely 262 pages and, as a book writer myself, I'm happy that the author found a reader.

Like the football in a football game (necessary but hardly significant), this little book isn't significant in itself. What is important, really important, is that it is there. It is there, along with millions of other books in our campus libraries, waiting for someone to need them.

Thank goodness that our libraries are there and are available for our use. Soon after I became provost, I attended a UNC system meeting about the future of libraries. Some expert consultants said that we would never build a new library on campus again, that the age of physical libraries was over. Everything we need will be available electronically, they said.

Consultants shovel a lot of manure (I know, I've been one), but this was among the deepest load ever. As exhibit one I submit that we recently spent $100 million to build the James B. Hunt Jr. Library and that it is filled to the brim with students at all hours of all days.

As exhibit two, I submit the little book about Operation Gwamba. Maybe, someday, someone will digitize that book, but don't hold your breath. Books and places like our libraries that care for them are still the greatest resource.

I've had the Operation-Gwamba experience many times in my career. I've searched for, found and checked out many books for which I was probably the virginal reader. Dozens of books that had been waiting for just the right time to be needed. Literal—and literary—wallflowers, waiting for an invitation to dance. My first significant journal paper was based on a series of British Royal Fisheries Commission reports from the 1800s, all lovingly preserved at the Cornell University library, waiting patiently for me. My early appreciation of conservationist John Muir came from reading his collected works, all held in a dozen or so matching volumes at the Virginia Tech library. And much of the background for two recent books I've published—*Provost* and *Nature's Allies*—came from books on the shelves of the NC State libraries.

Criticism of libraries comes cheap. Who ever reads those obscure books? What value are those highly specialized journals? Why do we subscribe to newspapers from around the world? In every budget cut that I've experienced in four decades of university life, and there have been many, one of the first moves has been to cut the library budget. The list of journals gets trimmed and the acquisition of new books gets chopped.

Libraries live on the edge partially because they have no alumni. Supporters of the university tend to focus on their degree homes, their fraternities and sororities, their clubs or their favorite sports. When it comes to donations or lobbying of the legislature, libraries are the runt of the litter.

They deserve better. As I learned from a book I borrowed from our library, Aldo Leopold, the father of wildlife management and author of the famous *Sand County Almanac*, believed that the most important tool of his field was not an ATV or good binoculars or a tranquilizer gun, but a good library.

We're fortunate at NC State because we have not a good library, but a great library. Great leadership, great staff, great facilities and great books. Don't take it for granted. I don't want us to ever need an Operation Gwamba to save our books from drowning in a rising lake of ignorance.

20

Almost the End of Free Expression

November 4, 2008 was an historic day in the United States. Barack Obama was elected the first African-American president of our nation.

November 5, 2008, was an historic day for North Carolina State University. Racist graffiti appeared on the walls of the free expression tunnel. It featured a caricature of President-Elect Obama accompanied by words similar to these: "Shoot the n-----."

Chaos followed. Almost before anyone had seen the writing, physical plant employees painted over it. Some had seen it, however, and they were angry. Perhaps most angry were the FBI and Secret Service—who had to treat this as a credible threat against the president-elect of the United States. Then came the protests from the African American community on campus, and soon after, from the leadership of the state NAACP chapter. The chancellor and I were in meetings almost immediately and for weeks afterward, as we attempted to calm emotions and fashion responses that would help, rather than hurt, the fragile situation.

Also almost immediately, the university identified the students who had done that disgusting and dishonorable "free expression."

(Surprise, surveillance cameras monitor the tunnel and dozens of other places around campus, so watch your step). The names of the students were never made public. Even as provost, I never learned their names. The threats being made against them *were* credible, and we lived for weeks in fear that the reactions would be worse than the original action.

No doubt the threat of violence to the president wasn't real, but the threat to the free expression tunnel was. In the weeks following the event, the university leadership talked behind closed doors about doing away with free expression. I lobbied hard for closure of the privilege of painting on the walls of the tunnel, arguing that its usefulness had passed. The chancellor wouldn't bite, however, being a lot savvier than me politically and a bit more hesitant to throw babies out with this filthy bathwater.

The chancellor was right; I was wrong. After all, the free expression tunnel is quite a traditional baby on campus. The tunnel was built originally in 1939, as a Works Progress Administration project. The WPA was one of the ideas of another ground-breaking president—Franklin Delano Roosevelt, also one much loved and much despised—designed to help pull the nation out of the Great Depression. As NC State had expanded south of the railroad tracks, more access between the two sides of campus was needed, and the WPA came to our rescue.

The WPA came to a lot of people's rescue. In North Carolina alone, in five years, the agency employed 125,000 people and completed nearly 4,000 projects. The swimming pool in Pullen Park and the Raleigh Little Theater were among them, along with the campus tunnel.

Fast forward 28 years, to 1967, when I was a college sophomore at the University of Illinois. Our nation's survival was again being threatened, but a failing economy wasn't the problem. The issues were bigger and broader—racial injustice, nuclear proliferation, the Vietnam War, the draft, women's rights, the sexual revolution. Universities were under attack from within, by their students and faculty.

The Free Expression Tunnel still carries important messages.

NC State students were part of that uproar, as well. And, apparently, one of their favorite pastimes was painting graffiti on walls around campus. The situation got bad enough that the Student Government proposed allowing the campus tunnel to be a permanent canvas for expressing anti-establishment feelings. The administration agreed, and on December 4, 1967, the Campus Welfare Committee passed regulations creating the Free Expression Tunnel. Students celebrated their new-found freedom with a "paint-in."

So, how "free" was the free expression when the tradition started? Not as free as you might think, especially when reading the messages that show up these days. Right from the beginning, the rules stated that vulgarity and obscenity were not allowed and "untasteful remarks" would be removed. It wasn't long before the inevitable debates started. The October 2, 1968 issue of *The Technician* carried a story decrying the sad state of free expression.[4] As late as 1995, the Chair of the Faculty Senate stated his displeasure: "My biggest concern is all the crude, crass and immature expressions. The good part is that we value free speech. I would just like to see enlightening and positive art instead."[5]

Ah, so would we all. I had grown pretty disenchanted with the free expression tunnel in the months leading up to November 5, 2008. It didn't seem to have the seriousness that it was created to express. In the late 1960s, free expression meant protesting against the Vietnam War. Today free expression meant promoting happy hour at local bars and celebrating your roommates birthday.

But I know it would be wrong to shut it down just because most of the free expression is trivial, vulgar or self-indulgent. Because when we have a need to express ourselves about something important, the free expression tunnel is always available, ready for the trivial to be painted over for essential messages. When tragedy strikes on campus, the free expression tunnel is there to provide therapy and community. When bad ideas surface on campus or around the world, the tunnel is there to battle back against them. When Chapel Hill needs a shellacking, the tunnel is there to shellac them with.

As an insightful student, Clayton Goldsmith, said a few years ago, "The Free Expression Tunnel is a book of sorts. New pages are written every day."[6] Some days the pages deserve to be read, some days they don't. Just like the newspaper.

21

Where's Waldo?

Our daughters loved the *Where's Waldo?* books that appeared in the late 1980s. They would search intensely, page after page, looking for the guy in the red-and-white striped shirt (no doubt, Waldo was a Wolfpacker). My favorite page was of the seashore, with people swimming, fishing, boating, scuba-diving—but, then, I am a fisheries scientist.

I'd like to suggest that NC State has its own Waldo. Actually an army of Waldo's. But, like Waldo himself, it is an almost invisible army. The members are hard to notice, literally and figuratively. They don't stand out in the crowd of students and faculty. They miss out on notoriety, busy doing their jobs under the cover of anonymity. You'll seldom hear their voices in the chorus of commentary about the university.

Just like Waldo would, they stand out the most when there is no one else around. Like during fall break, the long weekend in October when undergraduate students and most faculty members desert campus for home or shore or mountains. Campus seems pretty empty then, but you can find our invisible army hard at work, if you know where to look.

I was showing visiting relatives around during one fall break and took them, as I do with all visitors, to Hunt Library. I warned my guests that this wasn't a usual time, with students gone AWOL for a few days; I told them not expect to see anyone in the library.

But I was wrong. Sure, the library wasn't as crowded as usual, but there was still plenty of action. The group study rooms were mostly occupied, just with fewer students working together. The egg-pod chairs on the second floor were still all full. The quiet book room on the first floor was still packed.

What we were seeing was our wonderful army of graduate students, our Waldos. Literally they are almost invisible because they look the same as undergraduate students, dressed in the same leggings and t-shirts and denim as all the rest. Figuratively they are almost invisible because few people think of them as essentials parts of the university. Ask someone about students, and you'll most likely hear about our amazing undergraduate students. Ask someone about research, and you'll most likely hear about our distinguished, hard-working, entrepreneurial faculty members.

But mixed in with them is our impressive population of graduate students. NC State enrolls more than 9,000 degree-seeking graduate students. About half are women, a proportion that keeps growing every year. That's an admirably high proportion, given the intense science and technology focus of our campus (about one-third of all graduate students are studying engineering).

About 60% of graduate students are from North Carolina, a large proportion that is fed by the forward-looking economy of our state. Students from the Old North State want to stay here to take advantage of the Research Triangle and the high-tech job opportunities it provides. Another 30% or so are international, and the other 10% are from the other 49 states. A former dean of the Graduate School once told me that international students are a huge benefit to our university, including undergraduate students. "They add so much by allowing students to participate in a global community, even if they don't have the opportunity to travel abroad."

Graduate students, both domestic and international, contribute in many ways that are sometimes as invisible as Waldo. Graduate students take their own classes, of course, but that moves from a top priority for an undergraduate to a necessary-but-not-sufficient part of graduate school. First priority is the work they do as teaching or research assistants to keep bread on the table.

My last teaching assistant, Darya Cowick, was originally from Bulgaria, working on a Master's degree in forestry. She graded the papers I assigned, bless her heart. The 300 students in my class wrote 3 short papers each over the semester—so about 900 papers in all. Figure each paper requires 15 minutes to grade, and we're talking about 225 hours of grading. But the grading needs to be done fast, within a week or so, to keep students happy. So, Darya spent about 10 hours of grading per day for 7 straight days on each assignment, a mind-blurring and mind-blowing task. And Darya did this for three straight semesters, always with a smile. Bless her heart times three.

Lucky graduate students don't have to grade papers; instead, they get research assistantships, paid to work on their advisors' grant-supported projects. That embeds them into the core of the research endeavor of their discipline, the reason they enrolled in graduate school. More than embedded, they are essential. They do the grunt work of research. They count the bacterial colonies in the Petri dishes. They follow tagged bears around the woods. They record the behavior of children on playgrounds. Faculty members don't get to do that work as much as they'd like, because they are busy writing new grants, administering current grants and writing the papers needed for tenure. As the former dean said, "Without graduate students, our research grinds to a halt." Bless their hearts.

When the papers are graded and the bacteria are counted, graduate students get to work on their own thesis or dissertation research. Performing a significant research project is, of course, the essential difference between the undergraduate and graduate experience. It becomes an obsession, an addiction that demands to be fed, involving many months or many years of original thinking, observation, analysis, heart-break and, in the end, break-through. That's why, when most of us are off cavorting on fall vacation (or spring, Thanksgiving and Christmas vacation), graduate students stay hunkered down in a Hunt Library study room, working on that big nut they have to crack. They have neither the time nor the money to take breaks.

All in all, it's a big job, being a graduate student. Most students, however, love it. A few years ago, I was teaching a seminar to advanced graduate students about how to make a speech. Step one was brainstorming about the topic. Most of us have trouble brainstorming—just letting the ideas flow, without judging whether they are good or bad. So, for practice, I asked the students to start yelling out their first reaction to this question, "What is graduate school like?" After filling the white board with dozens of ideas in just a few minutes, a clear theme emerged. I circled two phrases on the board and wrote, "Graduate school—no time for sleep, but what a chance to dream!"

Waldo is out there, all around us at NC State. Thousands of graduate-student Waldos, anonymous but essential to the life of the university. Next time you discover Waldo, tell her thanks for grading your papers, for collecting your data, for keeping the university's wheels turning. But, if Waldo is sleeping, let her be—she's dreaming.

22

Hillsborough Street Redux

Hillsborough Street just finished a major make-over. For several years, the street was in chaos where it brushed past NC State. A conscientious student on the four-year plan might have come to campus as a freshman and graduated as a senior and never traveled the length of Hillsborough from Gorman to Ashe without running a mogul course of orange cones, missing pavement, metal plates and diverted lanes.

It was worth it, of course. The thoroughfare is much more attractive now, with buried utility lines, brick crosswalks and upscale bus-stop shelters. More efficient, too, with a series of traffic circles eliminating the need for stoplights—and creating confusion for the unsuspecting driver.

Pretending that the Hillsborough Street landscape has much in the way of permanence, however, would be pure fantasy. "Redux" is a euphemism for "change ahead!" Hillsborough Street is and always will be in a state of perpetual redux. Restaurants close before their grand-opening coupons expire. Old tattoo parlors and shabby bars become high-rise student apartments that block out the sun. A strip shopping center becomes the Aloft Hotel. The bowling alley becomes a Target. NC State programs squeeze into miscellaneous vacant storefronts, playing a game of hide-and-seek with their department heads.

Amidst all this upheaval, however, Hillsborough Street has some roses that deserve our stopping to take a smell. If Raleigh were a small town in England, say, a group of old geezers wearing blue badges would be offering walking tours, amusing and enlightening tourists with tales of past wars, famous and infamous characters, and colorful and insignificant events. So, take a walk with me down the street, and I'll explain why Hillsborough Street is remarkable in it's own right.

Our walk begins few blocks from campus, at the westernmost traffic circle. This is where Reader's Corner Used Books calls home. If you're out of reading material, this place has 70,000 volumes for your consideration, some costing just 25 cents. As Hillsborough retail establishments go, this place is Methuselah. Born in the mid-1970s, it has been selling used books at a slow, steady pace for nearly half a century. A unique feature is the store-long display of cheap books you see on those outdoor racks. They live there all day, everyday, protected marginally from the weather by that overhanging eave. All proceeds from selling these books go directly to WUNC radio. A few years ago I found a used copy of Rachel Carson's *The Edge of the Sea*, the book that I checked out of the library as a teenager and inspired me to become a fisheries biologist. Be careful in there—it could change your life![7]

Across Hillsborough Street and just a bit closer to campus is the Raleigh Nehi Bottling Company building. The building dates to the late 1930s, and it demonstrates an architectural fashion of the time called the 'international style.' The style stressed simplicity, still evident in the building's plain exterior covered with those flat black glass panels framing the door and a simple porch topped with a plain round red roof. When I arrived at NC State in 2001, the building was derelict, the façade crumbling and the glass panels cracked. The distinctive part of the building, I thought, was the mural on the west side that read, "I love Raleigh," accompanied by a spray of red hearts.

In the early 2000s, this image greeted drivers heading East on Hillsborough Street towards campus.

But that was a late addition to the building. The original mural has been restored, advertising Royal Crown Cola. You may know that Pepsi was invented in New Bern, North Carolina—but around here at one time, Royal Crown must have been king! And replicas of the original red lettering on the front of the building have been restored as well—"Raleigh Nehi Bottling Company." The city made it an historic site in 2010, as an icon of international style. If you ask me, it is a building only an architect could love. But since we have a fine design school at NC State, by golly, we're going to love it.[8]

NC State begins in earnest where Dan Allen tees into Hillsborough. There, on the north side of the street is a small building with an overhanging first-floor balcony. Officially, it's called "Building A." It's a good place to get out of the rain, but not for much else. Today it houses part of the Poole College of Management, most of which is across the street in Nelson Hall. When I arrived, the humble structure was the home of Multi-Disciplinary Studies, a department that purposely sought to belong nowhere and everywhere. Physically, they were nowhere—in Building A!

But the wall under the overhang deserves a closer look. A small plaque there reads, "SAS—The world's largest, privately-owned software company was established on this site on July 1, 1976." SAS was the brainchild of NC State faculty members Jim Goodnight and John Saul. In their offices in Building A they developed "statistical analysis software," a computer program that could calculate your data's means, standard deviations, variances, regressions and correlations. When I was completing my doctorate in those days, that program was the bee's knees. Using it was a bruiser, but if you conquered the inputs, the outputs were life-savers.

The rest of the world liked it, too, and Drs. Goodnight and Saul became our homegrown versions of Bill Gates. Their program launched the industry that we call "data analytics" today. In fact, because of their encouragement and vision, NC State began the first graduate program in Advanced Analytics anywhere in the world. SAS lives today on its own complex in Cary. Drs. Goodnight and Saul are both billionaires and among the most generous of our university's benefactors.

Back on the NC State side of the street stands an historical marker of particular relevance to the Wolfpack. The land where the bowling alley used to be (and where the Target store now beckons) and for many blocks on both sides was the home of North Carolina's

State Fair for half a century. From 1873 to 1925, the finest wares of the Old North State's farms, fields and forests were exhibited for all to see. But within that time frame, a particularly important event took place there.

It was the 1884 North Carolina Exposition.[9] Blow-out celebrations of civic pride were all the rage in the late 1800s, bracketed by the 1876 Centennial Exposition in Washington and the 1892 Columbian Exposition in Chicago. North Carolina got the itch for its own party, and instead of a state-fair in 1884, the state declared an "exposition." A massive temporary building went up, looking a lot like the state fair building now on Hillsborough Street at Trinity. Displays covered all the leading industries of the Old North State. People came, people went, but the economic boon expected from the exposition never occurred. However, one happy outcome did develop—a new institution, the North Carolina College of Agriculture and Mechanic Arts, was born three years later. Today we call it NC State.[10]

The last stop on our tour is Mitch's Tavern. Rivaling Reader's Corner for longevity, Mitch's Tavern lives up a narrow stairway at 2426 Hillsborough Street. Mitch Hazouri bought the place, then called "The Jolly Knave," in 1972 and soon renamed it after himself. He tossed out the gamblers, replaced the shag dance floor with foosball tables and started selling food. In the early 1980s, he added five television sets—and a campus monument was born. By the late 1980s, Mitch said, "We were the top Budweiser seller on the east coast, east of the Mississippi."[11]

History had a lot to do with the most famous event in the life of Mitch's Tavern. The producers of a low-budget movie rolled into town one day, looking for a bar as the backdrop for part of the film. They needed a joint that looked old, and Mitch's fit the bill. "We picked it because you can't just make a place look like it's been there for 80 years," the producers told Mitch. The movie, in case you've been asleep for the past generation, was *Bull Durham*. It might have started as a low-budget film, but it was a box-office smash in 1988 and continues to be one of the most popular baseball movies of all time. The success may be due more to the chemistry between Kevin Costner and Susan Sarandon, but I like to think Hillsborough Street added a bit to the mystique.

23

The Starting Line

On the sidewalk outside Withers Hall one day near the end of a recent August, I stopped to ponder what was written below my feet. A straight yellow line was drawn across the bricks. Above it was the word, "Start."

I suppose the line signaled the beginning of some student-led activity from the recent past, but to me it was an allegory for what was going on around me. That day, you see, was the start of the fall semester. The first day of classes. A banner hung on the railing outside Hill Library promising that "We're glad you are back!" And, by and large, we were. That was the sentiment all day, as random faculty passed my office and offered a greeting. "Happy new year!" smiled one. "Are you ready?" taunted another. "Get ready, Nielsen, they're coming!" menaced a third. Yessiree, it was all about to start.

What a contrast from two weeks earlier, when nothing, absolutely nothing, was happening on campus. Then the university had been taking a power nap. Second summer session had ended, and both teachers and students had skedaddled for one last trip to the shore or mountains.

The pulse of non-academic summer activities had stopped as well. Middle-school campers no longer swarmed over the playing fields, honing their soccer skills under the watchful eyes of assistant coaches earning some extra pay. No tight bands of teenagers tramped the campus in FFA jackets, hurrying to their next competition somewhere among the jungle of agriculture buildings. Nothing had been in session on the Court of Carolina—no one holding court, not even anyone courting. The volleyball beach between Owen and Tucker Halls had sat empty, the net hanging sadly, no doubt feeling like the boxed toys in the attic of *Toy Story*. Lonely bus drivers had stopped at empty corners, keeping carefully on schedule for their non-existent riders.

But not now. Any pretense of calm had evaporated. Most office door were open, faculty members reorganizing their courses, advisors solving scheduling problems, office staff keeping the wheels of the bureaucracy cranking.

The copy machine was happy, too, I supposed, eager to flex its photostatic muscles in support of syllabi, semester schedules and introductory handouts. Copy machines must go into a form of hibernation over the summer, electrons beating at a slow pace, lubricant pooling in the bottom of whatever it has where an oil pan should be. Getting roused to copy an occasional invoice or travel voucher must hardly take a flicker of effort. We had leased a new copy machine over the summer, installed while I was at the beach. Looked scary to me, all sleek and shiny and with rounded corners to protect absent-minded professors from bruises on their hips. It looked entirely too much like that commercial where the robot actually transforms into a copy machine. I asked one of our capable office assistants if it worked like the old one, whose various buttons and levers I had mastered through years of paper jams.

"Yep, just like the old one," I was assured. I entered my password successfully and the control panel sprang to life. "Liar," I shouted, "this looks like the cockpit of a jet airliner." With her able assistance, I managed to nurse it down the runway, and after being re-fueled with two reams of paper in mid-flight, it finally delivered 300 copies of my class schedule.

After that, I needed my walk around campus.

Campus seemed especially busy. The sidewalks were crowded, and I heard more "Hello, Dr. Nielsens" than usual. The first day of class gets everyone on the move, students afraid that if they miss the first session the instructor will drop them from the roster. I always fielded several emails from worried students on the days before classes begin, explaining why they won't be in class and begging me not to drop them (hey, I'm not that mean; after all, this isn't chemistry or engineering or public speaking).

The brickyard was in full swing. The campus preacher bellowed in full voice, no doubt having enjoyed the same sort of rest as our copy machine ("Good afternoon, Provost," he proclaimed, as he always did, even though I was well past my provost term). ROTC cadets were massing for some sort of formality, as their leaders struggled to get the raw recruits into straight lines of equal numbers. A crazed student on a skateboard was tempting fate with a combination of speed and maneuvering amid the pedestrians. A group was offering prizes for filling out surveys. And several other groups were seeking new members or selling donuts or pushing their advocacy to disinterested students.

So, after I paused to consider the "Start" line, I set out to detect its destination. I followed in the direction that it seemed to be leading—across in front of Patterson, then the library and down the street to Nelson and then down Dan Allen. But I never did find the finish line.

So I'm sticking to my allegorical interpretation. The finish line, I'm sure, would show up in mid-December, just after final exams.

24

Graduation through the Looking Glass

I heard him say it a million times. Excuse me, I exaggerate. I heard him say it exactly 15 times. "Please understand this, graduates," the dean said, "You are by far the best graduating class in the history of Virginia Tech's College of Agricultural Sciences." The students would erupt in hoots and hollers—they were, after all, aggies—and their parents would smile politely and applaud.

For seven and a half years as Department Head of Fisheries and Wildlife at Virginia Tech (2 graduations per year equals 15 total), I sat behind the dean, in rows with my fellow department heads, glad to be watching our students reach the finish line. For the first few years, I bristled at the dean's brazen assertion. How did he know they were the best? And how could he say it every time, just like the last time? Had he no shame? Eventually, I admitted that, in at least some purely technical ways—number of 4.0 GPAs, average time to graduation, percentage with jobs—he might be right. Even more importantly, he wasn't going to admit anything other than continuous improvement. We were great, and we were getting greater. That's our story, and we're sticking to it.

Then I realized that it was only a small group of insiders who ever heard him say those words more than once. Most of the folks in the auditorium were graduation rookies. The only repeat offenders were the department heads and associate deans who filled the stage behind the dean.

Redundancy is a common strategy of graduation dignitaries. No sense in discarding a good speech that no one in the primary audience has heard before. It was true during my time at Virginia Tech, Penn State and NC State. At a pre-graduation luncheon for our Wolfpack fisheries and wildlife students, I confided in one of my favorite students and her parents. Listen to the dean when she first starts speaking, I said, she'll admit to wearing a Carolina-blue robe because she has to—she earned her doctorate over on Franklin Street. Then she'll say, "But to show my true colors, I'm wearing my red shoes!" And she did, just like she had at every graduation during her term as dean. And the crowd laughed and cheered, just like always. That was her story, and she was sticking to it.

A quick and probably inaccurate calculation makes me guess that I've attended at least 70 college graduations. For most of them, I've been behind the looking glass—on the stage, looking out at the graduates and their families. What's it like from the other side of the cap and gown?

First, we have to get ourselves organized. The College of Natural Resources usually has its graduation in the big hall at the McKimmon Center, every May and December. Faculty members are told to get there thirty minutes early because parking is limited. Some of us actually followed the directions, but I usually showed up just minutes before the start of the event, even when I was dean. I had learned early on that a few parking spots lurked behind the building by the loading docks (don't tell anyone).

Graduation is a wonderful time, whether you are in front
of or behind the podium!

To get ready, we're assigned to assemble in the back hallway,
where we make fun of each other's "academic regalia" (that's the official name of the ridiculous get-ups we have to wear). One of our
crowd went to a British university, and he always showed up dressed
like the picture on a bottle of Beefeater Gin. Another had read the
official protocol on academic regalia and figured out he could wear a
dark-gray fedora rather than the usual flat-topped hat; he'd look like
a 1950s private detective if the hat didn't have a tassel hanging over
his right ear.

Then we have the processional. Someone starts playing a classical
march on a piano somewhere, and we're off. It's not elegant or co-
ordinated. We pretty much run up the aisle onto the stage. We've

learned to get to our seats quickly, because slow and stately just means longer until the diplomas got awarded.

The first half of most graduation programs include a bunch of unmemorable speeches. Most are short, thank goodness, and most are unmemorable. In the College of n natural Resources, three students (one from each department) give brief speeches. Graduation after graduation, these have been wonderful—personal, happy, sincere, and short.

Switching venues for a moment, let me describe one speech that was quite memorable. This was at the big university graduation held in the PNC Arena, back when it was the RBC Center. The speaker was the ultra-liberal talk-show host Phil Donahue. No one knew how liberal he was until he started talking. Graduation speakers are given a 12-minute limit and gently advised to talk to the new graduates about their futures. Donahue ignored the advice. His speech went on for 40 minutes and was aimed at ticking off everyone present. He called it, "Take a Liberal to Lunch," and proceeded to insult the government, military, patriotism (nothing wrong with burning the flag, he said) and if he'd had a few more minutes, he'd probably have taken on North Carolina barbecue. When it became clear we were in for a marathon, folks started acting up. A steady chorus of boos began; family members in the stands yelled for him to go to hell and stormed out. Graduates started walking out, before they got their diplomas. I was sitting directly behind Chancellor Mary Ann Fox, and I thought her oversized hat was going to blow off her head. Needless to say, we invited only carefully vetted uncontroversial speakers for the next decade.

Eventually, we get to the distribution of diplomas, what everyone has come for. As provost, one of my privileges included handing the diploma sleeves (no diplomas because that would be too confusing) to the doctoral candidates at the big university graduation.

The veterinarians were the most fun. They've cornered the market on clever decorations of their academic regalia. Many had inflated examination gloves pinned to their hats, homage to hours of being elbow-deep inside various animal body cavities. Some created miniature barnyards or zoos on their hats, others decorated with a favorite stuffed animal or perhaps just ears and a tail. One balanced a cage of live mice on her head (cute, but undoubtedly a violation of the animal care and use protocols).

Back in the College of Natural Resources, we have a great tradition to accompany the distribution of diplomas sleeves (no diplomas, of course, too confusing). For each department, the faculty members line up at the bottom of the stage where we shake hands with each new graduate as she or he comes past. We get our official chance to say goodbye, get a hug or a high five, and officially show that we love them.

The parade coming off the stage at one recent graduation was a reminder of all that's good in the university, no matter what side of the graduation looking-glass you're on. Here came a student who was so shy that she barely spoke as a freshman; by graduation she had led virtually every student activity in the college. Then came the disabled veteran who not only makes lemonade from lemons, but goes purposely looking for them. Here's one who has finally fought his way through chemistry and calculus, perhaps the proudest in the procession. Then came the 70-year-old who has been determined to get a degree and start, I don't know, maybe his fourth career. Then my advisee who has told me about every fish he'd caught since we met at freshman orientation. And the student who went with me to Costa Rica, her first trip outside North Carolina, and now intends to save the Amazonian rainforest, single-handedly if she has to. Here's the student-athlete who is both a student and an athlete.

Here's the one who will make me famous when she mentions me in her Nobel Laureate acceptance.

And then the truth hits me. The dean was right. This is the best graduation class ever.

25

May the Zen be With You

For several days during a recent May, my temporary home was the city of Busan, South Korea. I was there to deliver the opening address at the 7th World Fisheries Congress—invited for this honor because I had co-chaired the 1st World Fisheries Congress twenty-four years earlier. Busan, the second largest city in South Korea, is a modern metropolis stretching along the southern coast of the country.

Far removed from my usual lunch-time walks around campus, I substituted rectangular routes around several blocks of the city. Busan bustled with activity—this was, after all, modern-day Asia. Traffic whizzed by, guided by some Korean instinct that tells drivers when red lights mean stop or just mean slow down, honk and continue. People hustled along the sidewalks, pigeons demanded attention, construction crews created detours.

But there was something different about Busan from other cities I've explored around the world. Nearly every intersection provided a refuge from the fevered activity. The refuges varied from corner to corner. Perhaps a small grove of closely planted trees. Or maybe a covered platform surrounded by wooden benches and flower planters. Or a twenty-foot long stream with a water wheel. Or at least a small sculpture garden. Sometimes they were at street level, sometimes they were sunken down a flight of steps, providing even more tranquility and distance from the demands of the day.

I found myself stopping momentarily in most of these—and hence not making very good progress on my walk—to smell the metaphorical roses.

Mary Yarborough Court, between Wautauga Residence Hall and the Peele Building, is a rejuvenating spot on campus.

The NC State campus is just like Busan. The campus is sometimes dissed by visitors as, well, not very pretty. In an old review that ranked our campus as one of the ten ugliest in the country, it was described simply as "brick, brick, brick, brick, brick." Yeah, well, we like our bricks to be sure, but only seeing the bricks and the buildings and the parking lots is to ignore all the little places that give refuge, just like Busan's islands of green.

There's the Mary Yarborough courtyard behind Holladay Hall, for example, afire with daffodils in the spring and swathed in restive shade throughout the year. And the little green area between the Free Expression Tunnel and Williams Hall, complete with bench swings. Or the "woods" between Biltmore and Jordan Halls, the flower gardens in front of Scott Hall, and the student-inspired eco-zone between Owens and Alexander Residence Halls.

But the true gem of green rejuvenation is a couple of miles west of the main campus—J. C. Raulston Arboretum. I wish it were closer, so that we could all drop ion on our daily treks across campus rather than needing to plan a visit.

The Raulston Arboretum is considered one of the best university gardens in the country, not a bad result for a pretty new place, as botanical gardens go. The garden owes its origin, and its name, to James Chester Raulston, who joined our faculty in 1975 as a newly minted horticultural professor. He had an idea to start a garden, and engaged a landscape architecture student to draw up a plan as his Master's project. Raulston liked the plan and started planting. Pretty soon, on what was then called "Horticultural Plot 4," the university had an arboretum. Without asking for one, as it turns out. A colleague wrote later, "The university woke up one day and said, 'Where did this arboretum comes from?'"

It came from a modern-day Johnny Appleseed. Raulston roamed North Carolina—and the world—looking for plants that could diversify and beautify gardens in the Southeastern U.S. He was passionate about discovering, propagating and then distributing plants he thought worthy of being used. The horticultural director of the public Wave Hills Garden in the Bronx said Raulston was relentless in his mission: "At least once a year, we'd get a great big cardboard box of 100 plants we'd never seen before....His whole life was giving plants away and sharing." Many consider him the leading horticulturist for gardens in the last half of the 20th Century, and in the 1990s, awards started falling at his feet like maple leaves after a November rain.

The Japanese Garden at Raulston Arboretum is a refuge of peace and beauty.

He grew students and friends as well as plants. A bachelor, he converted a downtown-Raleigh warehouse into a place where he and visiting friends could stay. People came and went as they pleased. He died in a tragic car accident in 1996, leaving a legacy and a sadness that both remain.

He didn't ignore home as he was Johnny-Appleseeding his way around the world. Our arboretum now holds over 7000 plants, including the most diverse collection of woody plants anywhere in the country. Most came directly from Raulston's efforts. He lived and worked from a simple idea, with which he ended all his letters: "Plan and plant for a better world."

For me, the best part of the arboretum is the Japanese Garden. About halfway along the path that leads from the visitor's center is a small turnoff to the south. It curls around a wall and deposits you in an island of tranquility. If you ever need a figurative definition of Zen, go to the Japanese Garden and sit awhile—no dictionary needed. The surrounding wall separates the garden from the rest of the property, and from the rest of the world. Japanese maples and myrtles shade the single bench, elevated slightly on a wooden walkway. Most of the area is covered in small pebbles, usually raked into the elegant lines and swirls.

When I was dean and provost and in some extra need of escape, I would call Sharon and have her meet me in the garden with a picnic lunch. Seldom did a random wanderer or another refugee intrude on our reverie. We would chat a bit, of course, but mostly we sat and ate, absorbed by—nothing.

To be absorbed by nothing is a precious blessing. A blessing we all need, more often than we recognize. If you are in Busan and need a blessing, stop on any corner. If you are a Wolfpacker, stop at the arboretum. But do me a favor. If I happen to be in the Japanese Garden, just walk on by.

26

Pullen Park

Get close to the eastern edge of campus and you'll be sure to hear it—the unmistakable call of a steam whistle. Whoooo! Whoooo!

How many universities, do you suppose, can call a steam train their next door neighbor? Only one is my guess—NC State. How lucky can you get!

Pullen Park is our next door neighbor, right across—you got it—Pullen Road. The park is named for Richard Stanhope Pullen, a wealthy Raleigh merchant who lived from 1822 to 1895. Stanhope, as he preferred to be called, never married and, consequently, had a substantial fortune to lavish on his beloved Raleigh community. He donated the land for Pullen Park, a little more than 60 acres. He wanted the old cow pasture, as he called it, to achieve a higher purpose.

He also wanted the adjacent 60 acres to achieve a higher purpose. So he gave it to the state as the location for a new university—The North Carolina College of Agricultural and Mechanical Arts. Right, NC State. The border between the park and the university was laid out by mule and plow, under the direction of Stanhope himself, and became Pullen Road.

Pullen Hall—where you go to do self-righteous battle with Registration and Records—is named for him, but it is not the first building on campus with that name. The first Pullen Hall opened in 1902 and was located next to Peele Hall, where a parking lot sits today. The original building was right in the middle of campus in those days and served many purposes—auditorium, dining hall, and library. The first basketball game played on campus occurred in Pullen Hall in 1911. In one notorious prank, students locked a live black bear in the building to protest against mandatory church attendance. Perhaps as another act of protest, a student arsonist set the building on fire in 1965. The current Pullen Hall was built in 1987.

But I digress. Pullen Park is the subject of this story. Stanhope Pullen thought Raleigh should have a public park—so he gave the land, paid for the facilities and hired a Park Keeper. Established on March 22, 1887, Pullen Park became the first public park in North Carolina. He added a swimming pool—wooden!—in 1891. The first carousel opened in 1915, and the current carousel is a 1900 original that was moved from Pennsylvania to Pullen in 1921. The carousel is on the National Register of Historical Places, and it is a wonder. Restored in the early 1980s, it has 52 animals and 2 chariots to ride, a pipe organ that could shout down a rock concert, and it spins at a dizzying speed (ride at your vertiginous peril). With all the facilities in the park, it is designated as an "amusement park," the 14th oldest one in the world, according to the National Carousel Association Census, and they ought to know!

But it is the steam train that I love. When I walk the eastern perimeter of campus, the whistle on that steam train beckons me. "I hear the train a comin', it's rollin' 'round the bend," just like Johnny Cash sings. I follow Rocky Branch under the Pullen Road viaduct, then ford the Rocky Branch Creek on a conveniently spaced group of stones and head up the hill. I hope to catch a glimpse of the train as it comes round the bend and wave at the kids and their keepers—parents, grandparents and nannies—as they chug by. It's bright red and shiny, nostalgia pouring out of the chimney right along with the steam. We take our grandsons there almost every time they come to town. They've outgrown the little boats that spin in a circle around a tank, but not the train. Like Sheldon Cooper, we'll never outgrow the train.

The steam train in Pullen Park is always full of smiling, waving children—of all ages!

My walk then continues as a leafy journey back up towards campus, walking under the towering magnolias and oaks that Stanhope

Pullen planted for us a century ago. Sometimes I go the long way through the park, past the playground. It is always crowded with running, climbing, digging, swinging, sliding, laughing, joyous children. Then up the hill past the pavilions filled with school groups on outings, erupting with more joyous chaos.

Centennial Campus was designed to be a mixture of university and community, and we get lots of deserved credit for creating something so wonderful. But it seems appropriate to me that we recognize Richard Stanhope Pullen as the originator of that concept. And a great one it was. Whoooo! Whoooo!

27

Food, Glorious Food!

When I was an undergraduate, the standard I've-got-an-early-class breakfast was a Tab and a Snickers. Something for energy, something for caffeine. Lunch and dinner included one dish at each meal, take it or leave it. About the only thing you could get seconds of was bread. White bread. And maybe some jelly for it. Grape jelly.

I'm so glad it isn't those good ol' days anymore. Eating has become a joy rather than a refueling exercise. But I wasn't aware that NC State was leading the way until I noticed a poster outside Witherspoon advertising NC State as a place that promotes healthy eating and living. News to me, because I didn't use dining services often. Sometimes I went to Chick-Fil-A in the Atrium. The chicken strips are great, but the waffle fries are one of my favorite guilty pleasures. Love those waffle fries!

So, to catch me up on what has happened over the last 50 years in campus grub, I had lunch with Randy Lait, former Director of Dining Services, and Lisa Eberhart, former Director of Nutrition and Wellness (they have both retired from the university). We ate at the State Club, in the Park Alumni Center. The State Club started out as a private restaurant, but Dining Services now runs it, along with virtually all other dining facilities on campus. They operate about 40 individual dining locations that serve more than one million meals per year. Even the Chick-Fil-A franchise is owned and run by Dining Services.

And do we ever promote healthy eating and living! NC State signed up in 2014 with the Partnership for a Healthier America, one of Michelle Obama's signature initiatives. We were among the first college campuses in the country to accept her challenge to do things differently than a diet soda and a candy bar. And did we ever do things! Our first annual report to Mrs. Obama, for 2015, ran to 13 pages. It included 23 specific items that we committed to get done in three years, by 2017, everything from providing free water at dining halls to providing physical fitness trainers for students.

And we aced this test. We completed all the requirements *in less than a year*, becoming the first university in the nation to do so. Along the way, we've been recognized as the 15th healthiest college in the country, the 4th best university accommodating gluten-free diets, and the 31st best college dining experience. I wish this were an ACC sport, because we'd be the champions!

How did this happen? On purpose was Randy's answer. And he should know. Before he retired in 2020, he had been at NC State his entire career, including as an undergraduate student. He started working for dining services as a 17-year-old and racked up 36 years in dining, including running the place, before hanging up his apron.

In April, 2009, campus dining moved from student affairs, where it had been slogging along in a comfortable rut, to the new Campus Enterprises operation. The new arrangement challenged Randy and his folks to escape their rut. "We got good at food," he said.

Getting good at food meant many changes. Job One was getting the right folks involved. They went from employing one professionally trained chef to now having more than two dozen. With those skills available, the dining halls greatly decreased their serving of preprocessed foods and amped up "scratch cooking." The meals got better and more nutritious. By cooking more from scratch, the university became able to use more local products—one-quarter of all ingredients are sourced in North Carolina, and we actually grow some of our own products at the Lake Wheeler experimental farms.

Randy also hired Lisa Eberhart as dining's full-time dietitian. She had been advising the entire university on diet and nutrition, including athletics and catering (athletics needed two full-time dietitians to replace her). Lisa is a culinary treasure, with a full menu of awards and honors to prove it. With Lisa in place, a new era began; her goal was to make NC State "the healthiest place in the U.S." She introduced technology to manage their entire process, from raw ingredients to recipes to menus and dietary information for diners.

Consequently, the dining staff can make better decisions about their products. Take allergens, for example. Watching the trends that showed more children having allergies, Lisa knew that we had to get smarter about how we managed allergens as those children became college students. Our dietary technology now allows dining staff to immediately tell diners—on electronic message boards and phone apps—what is in the food they are serving. If they run out of one dish and substitute another, the information switches in real time. No one ever gets an unwelcome, maybe dangerous, surprise.

The technology works other magic, as well. For example, the system revealed that by switching to a gluten-free barbecue sauce, they could make an additional 38 dishes gluten free. And the gluten-free barbecue sauce cost less. Win-win-win!

It all seems to be working. Student evaluations of their dining experiences keep rising. "We met our goals for almost all our dining locations," said Randy, smiling. Students have substituted water for soft-drinks at an astounding rate—71% now list water as their preferred drink.

Tell me a secret, I asked Randy and Lisa. They answered together, "Grilled cheese." Turns out that grilled cheese sandwiches are a favorite lunch item for students, served virtually everywhere, every day. We had been making grilled cheese on white bread, but for the celebration of whole-wheat-bread week, we switched, without telling anyone. Since no one noticed, we've just kept on using whole-wheat bread—healthier and more nutritious. My mom was devious like that, sneaking things like zucchini into her breads and carrots into her cakes.

And mom is relevant to campus dining. When I asked Randy what the big difference is between student dining a generation ago and now, his answer was, "We've gotten rid of Mom." In the past, dining halls tried to replicate Mom's cooking, because that's what students were used to. Today, however, they expect a restaurant experience. Mom doesn't cook as much as she did then, and families eat out a lot. So, students expect high quality and lots of selection. "Customization is the new trend," Lisa said, for example, at wok stations where students can tell chefs what ingredients they want in their stir-fry.

The lack of cooking experience at home has also expanded the role of dining services. "Our mission," Randy said, "is really to help students lead long, healthy and productive lives." So, for example, dining services offers cooking classes. Reality shows have made cooking cool, but most students are pretty helpless in the kitchen. When students graduate and hit the cold, cruel world, we want good eating habits to stay with them. Cooking classes are so popular, Lisa said, "that they fill up about five minutes after we post them."

With NC State now leading other schools around the country in nutrition, I wondered if there was much more we could accomplish. So I asked what's the one biggest change we could do to improve the nutrition of students? Lisa didn't hesitate: "Switch the standard serving of waffle fries at Chick-Fil-A from medium to small."

Bummer.

Here's a little PS. Being a good land-grant university, one of NC State's overall goals is to create jobs and economic activity,. Lisa and Randy exemplify one aspect of this. They created a private company, Menu Analytics, that offers the strategies and tools they developed at State to other institutions. Because of a 2018 USDA regulation requiring accurate nutrition labeling on menus, the need for Lisa and Randy's expertise is now nationwide. Go Pack!

28

The Surrey Tree

Whenever I tour guests around campus, I always take them past my tree. The tree is a European beech, *Fagus sylvatica*. It lives on the front lawn of Holladay Hall, on the site of a massive oak that had to be removed several years ago. The tree was positioned there precisely, so that as it grows into its own massive hulk, it will frame one side of the Bell Tower as seen from the entrance portico of Holladay Hall.

I call it my tree, unofficially. Officially, it is a present from the University of Surrey in Guildford, England. Here's the official story.

About 15 years ago, Sir Christopher Snowden, then the head of the University of Surrey, decided he'd like a partner university in the United States. He did some research, looking for universities that shared his institution's traits—primarily a STEM school, expert at undergraduate teaching but with a sweet tooth for research and graduate students, and with a commitment to economic development and community involvement. He put NC State on his list of several promising schools, packed his bags and came across the pond to find a mate.

His itinerary had NC State as his first visit, probably because we have a direct flight between London and Raleigh. That was good luck for us. After a couple days of speed-dating, Vice-Chancellor Snowden declared this was love at first sight, cancelled the rest of his trip and headed home with a firm pre-nuptial (universities call such things Memoranda of Agreement). I could describe all ways our two schools are compatible, but perhaps this tells the story best: A prominent piece of campus sculpture at Surrey is a pack of three wolves running across a hillside!

NC State's partnership with the University of Surrey in England was pre-ordained: Public art on their campus features a trio of wolves!

From then on, the job of making this marriage work rested pretty much in my hands as provost. Figuratively, of course, since most of the real work was done by our Vice-Provost for International Affairs, Bailian Li. We've spawned a handsome family of Surrey-State off-spring in the intervening years. Joint faculty research projects, joint graduate degree programs, student and faculty exchanges, interdisciplinary symposia on one campus or the other. Our London study abroad program is a direct outcome of our Surrey-State connection.

Our partnership has been so successful that it has morphed into what is now the University Global Partnership Network. Initially just our two universities, the network now includes the University of Sao Paulo in Brazil and the University of Wollongong in Australia.

Ok, great, we have a friend in England. So where does my tree come in?

The University of Surrey campus is beautiful. The buildings are pretty ordinary, and they're all crammed together in a labyrinth that resembles a dense construction of yellow Lego bricks. Way-finding is a challenge; I needed GPS to find their Starbucks. But those buildings sit within a beautiful setting, made more beautiful because all the buildings are crammed together in a small space—no sprawl there.

Particularly breathtaking is the small campus lake, surrounded by large shade trees and flowering ornamentals. The campus is, in fact, a registered arboretum, with a dazzling array of specimens from around the world.

On one October trip to Surrey to teach part of an environmental management course, I arrived very early. The flight from RDU landed in London at dawn, the immigration lines were short, and my shuttle from Heathrow Airport to Guildford made record time. The driver dropped me at the entrance to the main administrative building, but the doors were locked and the offices dark. Nothing to do for the next hour except commune with nature.

I walked down to the lake and scraped the frost from a wooden bench. The autumn chill invigorated me after a cramped and sleepless overnight flight. The leaves of maple trees blazed in brilliant orange, weeping willows dripped their arched branches down to the water surface. The birds were singing with enthusiasm—just them and me there to appreciate the early morning beauty.

I sat absorbed in the tranquil beauty that is part of living and working on a college campus. Most urbanites seek parks and green space as a refuge from their normal lives and jobs. But we enjoy such refuge as our natural habitat.

As I reflected on that wonderful reality, an idea began to form. What better way to celebrate the partnership of two schools with beautiful campuses than by giving each other the gift of long life and beauty—the gift of trees.

About two years later, on March 30, 2016, we renewed our vows by exchanging trees. In what I claim was the world's first two-continent, two-campus, outdoor tree-planting teleconference, we simultaneously "planted" our trees. I represented NC State at Surrey, and Vince Emery, their Vice-Chancellor for International Affairs, represented Surrey on our campus. At the same moment—three o'clock in the afternoon at Surrey and ten o'clock in the morning outside Holladay Hall—we unveiled the plaques mounted at the bases of two trees. Our gift to Surrey was a tulip poplar, and their gift to us was a European beech.

Alas, like most good stories, this, too, has an element of sadness.

About a year later, Tom Skolnicki, our fine university landscape architect, stopped his bike when he saw me one afternoon on my campus walk. He took off his helmet and looked at me with forlorn eyes. "Bad news," he said. "The Surrey Tree is dying."

Living symbols of long-lasting partnerships have a tragic flaw—they are mortal. Our European beech was succumbing to a phyto-patho-something found throughout the Holladay Hall lawn area. I had watched the leaves turning yellow and falling off, but I hoped this was just a reaction to dry weather or heat. Not so. It was a goner.

The second Surrey Tree, standing tall, healthy and
straight, graces the lawn in front of Holladay Hall.

My choice, Tom told me, was to plant a different species that
wasn't susceptible to the pathogen in the original spot or plant a European beech someplace else. The decision was easy—plant something else right back in the original hole.

Cue the upbeat music! So we now have a new, improved Surrey
Tree. Tom planted a sweetgum, *Liquidambar styraciflua* 'Hapdell',
a new variety that doesn't drop those pesky spiked pods. It looks
to be a sturdy specimen that will hold up to any insult our soil or
weather might hurl its way. I've watched it for several years now, and
it is a fine stripling of a tree.

And for the record, I've since visited the tulip poplar planted on
the Surrey campus. It is doing well, too, growing like a weed.

Next time you are showing someone the Bell Tower, take a moment to cross the street and meet the Surrey Tree on the Holladay Hall lawn. Give it a hug for me!

29

A Tale of Two Libraries (in Two Cities)

Here's an SAT-type question for you (just in case you are nostalgic for the experience):

The British Library is to Magna Carta as the D. H. Hill Library is to what?

(1) The Declaration of Independence
(2) Wolfpack Fight Song
(3) Constitution of the United States
(4) Universal Declaration of Human Rights

Think about it for a while. I'll get back to you with the answer.

For four summers, I helped extend the NC State campus from Raleigh to London, England. As I mentioned in the Surrey Tree story, a London study-abroad program was one outcome of our partnership with the University of Surrey. We had originally planned to house the new program in Guildford, where Surrey is located, but eventually came to our senses: why put a program 30 minutes from London when it could *be* in London.

Each summer starting in 2013, several NC State faculty members have taken about 40 NC State students to London for a five-week period, typically covering all of July and a couple of days leaking into June and August. The courses rotate—usually sociology and arts or literature courses, maybe one about the environment and then maybe something different, like organic chemistry or materials engineering. I taught my primary course, Conservation of Natural Resources, for the four years I was part of it.

An odd place for a conservation course, you might be thinking. But London, one of the world's greatest cities, offers great opportunities for understanding natural resources. Consider the Royal Botanical Gardens at Kew, a fine place to observe biodiversity. Kew has about the best of everything attached to roots, from formal gardens to wild spaces, from cactus houses to the world's biggest lily-pads, from stands of bamboo to stands of redwoods. But for a biodiversity lesson, the most special exhibit is their specimen of the Wollemi pine, an Australian tree thought to be extinct for millions of years and then discovered alive in the 1970s. Intrepid Aussie botanists found it, and a few special places around the world, like Kew, now cultivate it with the goal of removing it from the list of the world's "critically endangered species." Thank goodness for such special people and places.

I walked the students for miles around Kew, treating them to tea and scones in the beautiful Orangery just before exhaustion overtook us. I had been saving the Wollemi pine to the end—the best for last. Importance doesn't always equate to a wow-factor, however. The Wollemi pine is an ordinary looking tree about 20 feet high, growing by itself without fanfare in an open lawn. Kew visitors who stick to the paved paths probably just walk by without noticing. But I made our class walk to the tree, stop, look and listen as I expounded on its importance. Nonetheless, one particularly courageous student said what his classmates might have been thinking: "This is what we've been waiting for? This dinky tree? THIS??"

Nc State students studying natural resources in London visit one of the world's great conservatories, Kew Gardens.

Other London opportunities were more visually impressive. A cruise down the Thames River focused on water resources, including the world-famous Thames Barrier for flood control and a stop at Greenwich Observatory to stand with one foot each in the eastern and western hemispheres. An all-day excursion to Stonehenge gave the opportunity to discuss World Heritage sites at one of the world's most amazing and mysterious protected areas. At the Brazilian Embassy, we met with specialists to discuss deforestation of the Amazon rainforest. We volunteered for a day at an urban nature center, rebuilding trails and clearing invasive plants. We rode the train to Cambridge to meet the leader of the International Whaling Commission and have lunch at The Eagle, the ancient pub where Watson and Crick announced their discovery of the double helix.

Another of the great resources of London—and one that doesn't generally get onto the schedule for most visitors—is the British Library. No, not the British Museum, with all those mummies and the Rosetta Stone, but the British Library. The display room at the library is the written-word equivalent of the world's best art museums (take your pick—the Louvre, National Gallery, Gregg Museum).

Want to see Charles Darwin's original notes about the origin of species? It's on display at the British Library. How about Sir Isaac Newton's original algebra proofs? Yep, that's there, too. Something composed by Beethoven? Check. Canterbury Tales in the original olde English? By Geoffrey, yes! And maybe something really important, like John Lennon's scribbled lyrics to "Strawberry Fields?" Yes, it's there, too, eight days a week.

And Magna Carta? Yes, the British Library has that, too. Remember, Magna Carta is the 1215 document that more-or-less established the principles of democracy. Mean King John was getting on the nerves of the other nobility, and they decided to put the screws to him. So, they wrote a series of demands—Magna Carta—and made him sign it. Lots of good stuff is in Magna Carta, most importantly the right to a trial by a jury of peers, based on the rule of law rather than the divine right of kings.

Only four original copies of Magna Carta survive today. The British Library has one, on display. It is a bit difficult to read, given that the original text is written in tiny, faded Latin script. We paid a lot of attention to Magna Carta while we were there (including learning that the name of it isn't "The" Magna Carta, but just Magna Carta). It was especially a focus in 2015, the 800th anniversary of its signing on June 15, 2015. In recognition of how important modern technology is to the freedom of expression, the British

Library also displayed a hand-stitched tapestry of the entire text as displayed in Wikipedia, 5 feet wide and 42 feet long.

London is one of the world's greenest cities, and our students helped keep it that way during a workday at an urban nature center.

About 733 years after Magna Carta was signed, the United Nations enacted the Universal Declaration of Human Rights, on December 10, 1948. The declaration, as the United Nations says, "sets out, for the first time, fundamental human rights to be universally protected...." It contains a preamble and 30 articles in 1778 words.

While I was provost, on each December 10, university leaders stood on the steps outside the southeast corner of D. H. Hill Library and took turns reading the Declaration, from beginning to end. The event was organized by what is now the university's Office for Institutional Equity and Diversity. The readers were pretty much ignored as students and faculty walked past, intent on their next class or meeting, or whatever was happening on their cellphones. But I loved the symbolism of the event. We were doing this because it was right, not because the world would notice. A verbal equivalent of viewing the Wollemi pine.

As Provost, I had the honor of reading the Preamble. Here is the final clause:

> *Now, Therefore THE GENERAL ASSEMBLY proclaims THIS UNIVERSAL DECLARATION OF HUMAN RIGHTS as a common standard of achievement for all peoples and all nations, to the end that every individual and every organ of society, keeping this Declaration constantly in mind, shall strive by teaching and education to promote respect for these rights and freedoms and by progressive measures, national and international, to secure their universal and effective recognition and observance, both among the peoples of Member States themselves and among the peoples of territories under their jurisdiction.*

How fitting, I've always thought, that an institution like NC State, which strives to teach and educate, has created a tradition around recognizing the equal humanity of every person. Nothing else matters, only that we are all human beings, linked together at our very core, regardless of all the sub-divisions that tend to drive us apart. Discrimination according to some characteristics—race, religion, age, gender—are prohibited by law. But most aren't covered by law, traits like personality, body shape, or even grade-point-average. All that really matters, however, is that each of us is human, no more or less human than any other.

Elie Wiesel, holocaust survivor, Nobel laureate and author of *Night*, was asked about how someone earned his respect. But he said, no, respect wasn't earned. You deserved respect just because you were a human being, not because you were good or sensitive or caring or had done me a good turn. He said that all human beings are the same and deserved to share basic human rights.

Reading the declaration on the library steps at NC State has been replaced by a new tradition. The provost has made a video with students and other leaders that is posted online. I understand that, of course, for lots of good, practical reasons—including its availability to all students all the time. But I still like the old tradition, when we stood up and read, even if no one seemed to be listening. It is, after all, what one does when no one is listening that defines one's character.

And so, back to the SAT question. If you answered (d), you are correct. What the British and D. H. Hill Libraries have in common is their backdrop for two of the most important documents in history, Magna Carta and the Universal Declaration of Human Rights. Thousands of miles separate the libraries and hundreds of years separate the documents, but the essential point remains the same: Each of us matters.

30

Wolves Aren't Endangered Here

When I arrived at NC State in August, 2001, you could hardly find a wolf anywhere. But that formerly endangered species is doing just fine on our campus now.

Wolves are everywhere. They guard the entrance to the Park Alumni Center. They're climbing a big rock in front of the Murphy Center at Carter-Finley Stadium. Chain-saw-art wolves grace the center of the Wolfpack Village grounds. They climb the stairs in the gloriously remodeled Reynolds Coliseum, and a giant wooden wolf fills one wall of the five-story lobby in Talley Student Center. And three strapping wolves prowl around the south entrance to the Free Expression Tunnel, the place we now call Wolf Plaza.

The wolf renaissance began with an explosion of fiberglass wolves in the fall of 2001. The Raleigh Arts Commission thought to replicate similar events that used cows in Chicago, moose in Toronto and pigs in Cincinnati. Raleigh artist (and NC State alum) Kyle Highsmith sculpted the body of the wolf; about 100 fiberglass forms were fabricated. Then artists and others decorated wolves to meet their artistic fancy and placed them around town. Most are gone now, but one, commissioned by the College of Natural Resources, still guards the entry to the Natural Resources Library in Jordan Hall.

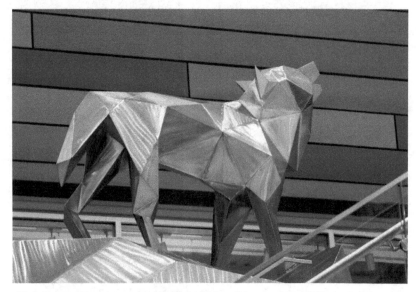

Wolves are all over campus now, including this gleaming fellow climbing the stairs in the wonderfully renovated Reynolds Coliseum.

Next came the "Wolfpack Turf" sculpture dominating the plaza in front of the Murphy Center. The 21-foot high stone mountain is home to a pack of wolves created by famed wildlife artist Dick Idol. Idol played football for the Wolfpack, part of the renowned "white shoes defense" that beat Georgia 14-7 in the 1967 Liberty Bowl. More importantly, he earned his degree in wildlife biology, his true love. Forsaking an NFL career, Idol followed his passion to become a wildlife entrepreneur, building a business enterprise from guiding to outdoor writing to broadcasting and, eventually, to art.

Each of the wolves proudly prowling the sculpture is twice life size and represents a quality of NC State athletes: confidence, passion, spirit, courage, pride and strength. Passion stands on the top of the mountain, I guess as the pinnacle of excellence.

My personal involvement with campus wolves relates to the trio in the Wolf Plaza. They started as a competition for an art installation at that location, as part of the major campus improvements made over the first decade of the century. We held an open competition for artists to submit their ideas for a commission to get some wolves on the main campus. A faculty-staff committee narrowed the choice down to three. Then the chancellor, chief financial officer and I, as provost, made the final selection.

Perhaps this wolf in Wolf Plaza is howling with joy because a snowstorm canceled classes?

Luckily for campus, we choose well. The wolves are spectacularly popular—and spectacularly artistic. We choose San Diego sculptor Michael Stutz (alas, not an NC State alum) to produce this small pack of wolves. Stutz uses strips of bronze to form his otherwise highly realistic forms. As a university news release described the installation in April 2010, the style "allows his creations—whether hawk or horse, man or wolf—to soar. His artwork is porous, open to the world, reflective and conductive of light, and almost fragile for all its tensile strength."

Those wolves are now part of the NC State persona. We've named the area where the wolves prowl as Wolf Plaza. Graduating students pose there in caps and gowns to commemorate their achievements. Students rally around the wolves to protest one thing or another, recruit new members to their clubs, and celebrate happy events.

31

Donuts for 300

Class was about ready to start at 8:30 AM. I was busy getting the technology set up in 232A Withers. With a class of nearly 300 students, technology is an absorbing necessity. Log into the computer, load the Powerpoint, cue the music, lower the twin screens, sound-check the microphone, make the incomprehensible lights work. I heard a commotion and looked up.

Down the aisle came a parade of my colleagues—department head, dean, a dozen or so faculty and staff, and my wife. They each carried several boxes of Krispy Kreme donuts. Tom Gower, my department head, started talking. Although this wasn't my last class, it was my last course before I retired. He thought a little party was in order.

I was floored. Speechless. I didn't hear much of what Tom said. The students stood and applauded, for a long time. I introduced my wife, Sharon, who students knew well as she-who-must-be-obeyed. My colleagues served donuts up and down the aisles—donuts for 300. It was a wonderful event, mostly because it was totally unexpected, a surprise to a guy who doesn't get surprised much. I barely managed to hold it together. My colleagues and wife left, and I got back to work. At least I think so, because I've no recollection of what I said for the next hour.

Why donuts, you ask. On my office wall hung a plaque containing a freeze-dried cake donut awarded to me as "The Departmental Donut" in 1994 by the graduate students in my department at Virginia Tech. It is a real donut, and it has survived for over a quarter century; graduate students studying the physiology of wild animals know how to preserve organic tissue. As their department head, I encouraged graduate students to finish their degrees completely—that is, thesis or dissertation signed off and accepted by the Graduate School—by treating them all to donuts each time a student finished. And for a completed dissertation, I bought jelly-filled donuts. Our graduation rate skyrocketed for several years. The plaque is one of my prized possessions.

All those donuts got me thinking about other memorable events in my classrooms over the years. Here are a few.

Best student-athlete. NC State swimmer Ryan Held took my class in Spring 2015. After he and his teammates won the NCAA championship in the 400-yard freestyle relay, we recognized him in class with rousing applause. Look in the dictionary under "great student-athlete," and you should see Ryan's picture. He later won an Olympic Gold Metal, and I beamed when he let me hold it with him for a picture. He sat in the right rear of the classroom, a spot often picked by other soon-to-be-famous athletes, including first-round draft picks Carlos Rodon (pitcher for the White Sox) and Dennis Smith Jr. (point guard for the New York Knicks). Seems like studying natural resources is good for your pro career.

Coolest prop. I always tell new teachers to use props in class. Anything works—juggling balls, costumes, antiques. But snakes are the best. Snakes are great examples to show the different way people feel about nature. Some like them, some hate them—and a full array of attitudes in between. For my second class period of the semester in my conservation of Natural Resources course, I usually arranged for a student to bring their pet snake in to make that point. The bigger the snake, the better. Until the semester when three male students brought a 12-foot reticulated python. It took all three of them to hold it. We challenged each other, that python and I, nose to nose, eye to eye. It flicked its forked tongue towards me playfully, as if to say, "Want a hug?" I blinked first.

Ryan Held, NC State champion swimmer, epitomizes the ideal of the student-athlete (and not just because he let me hold his Olympic Gold Medal).

Favorite active-learning task. A class of nearly 300 students doesn't invite much class participation. Groans at my bad jokes were about the limit. But, September 1, 2014 was different. That day was the 100th anniversary of the extinction of the passenger pigeon, when the last living member of the species, Martha, died at the Cincinnati Zoo. To raise awareness for the conservation of biodiversity, a national group organized an attempt to fold 1 million origami passenger pigeons. At NC State, we folded 1500, starting with 500 in my class. We held a birthday party for Martha on the Brickyard where students folded the rest. Teaching several hundred students to do origami is a lot more challenging than teaching them the logistic model for population growth.

Most famous TA. Nothing helps raise your teaching ratings like a good teaching assistant. I hit the jackpot when Justin Robinson joined me as a teacher for two semesters. Justin was a founding member of the Carolina Chocolate Drops, which won the Grammy in 2010 for the best traditional folk album. He can fiddle like nobody's business. When things got slow in class, I'd ask Justin to bring in an instrument—violin, guitar, whatever—and sing a song. A favorite was "Butcher Bird," comparing love gone wrong to the habits of the predatory Loggerhead Shrike, which impales its prey on a thorn before devouring it. My analysis shows that Justin was good for +0.2 points on the teaching evaluation.

Best excuse. I appreciate creativity in all its forms, but although students might think their excuses are original, an experienced teacher seldom hears anything new. My car broke down, the printer ate my paper, I needed to take my dog to the vet. My two favorite excuses were unique. A student called me the night before an exam. He said, "I was in jail all weekend and didn't have my notes, so I couldn't study. Can I take the exam late?" My answer, of course, was no. Many years later, a non-traditional student, a single mother with three children at home, emailed me. "All my kids got the flu," she said, "one right after the other. Can I take the exam late?" My answer, of course, was yes.

Most inspirational student. My first summer teaching in London, we enrolled a student who uses a wheelchair to get around. Her name was Xuan Troung. I thought her presence might be difficult to manage; England, despite what it might advertise, isn't as accessible to mobility challenged persons as the U.S. But Xuan was an inspiration, not a problem. She figured it all out, and so did her classmates. Her motorized chair took her many places, and she developed strategies for conquering the labyrinth called the London Underground. A smaller manual chair served for field trips. If we hit an obstacle, two classmates would grab the sides of the chair and in seconds she and we would be over it. Nothing stopped her. At Stonehenge, I lost her for awhile. Then I saw her, in the middle of an adjacent pasture, cruising among the sheep. Xuan has graduated and now works for an organization that helps differently-abled students go on study abroad.

Friends sometimes ask if teaching the same course over and over, semester after semester, got boring. Not for me. Each class brought new adventures with new and interesting students, and, occasionally, a few left-over donuts.

32

The Last Lecture

(The Last Lecture is a program at NC State and other colleges around the country in which students ask a few retiring professors each semester to give their thoughts about life to an audience of students, staff and faculty. I was honored to be invited to give one of the three presentations at our university's first celebration of The Last Lecture, on April 17, 2017. Here, more or less, is what I said.)

As a society, we are awash in advice. Ten ways to save money at the grocery store. A dozen apps everyone should have on their phone. Twenty things to do before you leave college.

Old people like me aren't exempt. Ten mistakes people make when they retire. Five signs that you are getting senile (or maybe it was ten—I can't remember). I own a book entitled, *1000 places to see before you die*. This, my wife tells me, is my job jar for retirement.

One of the pieces of advice we often get is what we should read. For generations, the idea of the "100 greatest books" has floated around. You need to read this and that in order to be considered educated. There are even books that provide short synopses of the 100 greatest books, so you can just read one book and appear educated. I'll bet there's an app for that, too.

Here's my advice: Forget about those lists that include "Balzac and Shakespeare and all those other highfalutin' Greeks," and do what Thoreau said, "Simplify, simplify." About 30 years ago, a book was published with the title, *All I really need to know I learned in Kindergarten.* I don't think you can simplify quite that much, but you can get close. You just need a few years of elementary school and the advice of one of the greatest philosophers of all time—one Theodor S. Geisel. In other words, everything you need to know, you can learn from Dr. Seuss.

So, today, let me give you seven easy lessons to learn from Dr. Seuss.

First off, his penname shouldn't be pronounced the way we all do. Seuss is his real middle name, it's of Germanic origin, and it's properly pronounced "zoice," like voice. He obviously got over the world pronouncing his name wrong, because about 7.4 billion of us know him as Seuss. So, there's Lesson 1: Don't take yourself too seriously. I mean it, seriously. There is nothing more wonderful than a person who can laugh at herself or himself—and nothing more boorish than a person who can't.

Seuss always made his living drawing pictures and writing stories. He started out as a commercial artist. He had a longtime arrangement with Standard Oil. His big hit for them was a series of cartoon ads for the popular insecticide called "Flit." His cartoons showed people beset in one way or another by insects, always accompanied with the line, "Quick, Henry, the Flit!" That line became a common idiom in the 1930s and 1940s for seeking help in an emergency.

He was highly successful, but he was getting tired of the advertising grind and wanted to write more serious stuff. Unfortunately, he had agreed to an airtight exclusive contract with Standard Oil. Seuss often said that he chose to write and illustrate children's books because that was the only kind of writing that his contract didn't forbid. So, there's Lesson 2: Always read the fine print. A different way to say that is: If you don't know where you are going, you'll probably end up someplace else.

A newly independent Seuss started writing children's books and the rest, as they say, is history. Well, not quite. It wasn't that easy. His first book, *And To Think That I Saw It On Mulberry Street*, was published in 1937. But here's the interesting part—it was rejected by 26 publishers before someone took a chance! Imagine that. Twenty-six times he slipped his manuscript into a manilla envelope, glued on some stamps and mailed it to publishers. An author who's sold more than 600 million books was turned down 26 times for his first book. So much for good judgment in the editorial suite! So, and you know it is coming, there is Lesson 3: Don't give up. Don't ever give up. Let's see, who else said something like that? Oh, yeah, Jim Valvano.

My recent book, *Nature's Allies*, profiles the lives of eight great conservationists who changed the world. Some are pretty famous, like John Muir and Rachel Carson; some are less famous, like Native American fisherman Billy Frank Jr. and Kenyan tree-planter Wangari Maathai. But none of them ever gave up. They all persevered. They didn't change the world in one day, but they got there. Dr. Seuss persevered, and he changed the world. And you should persevere, too, and maybe you can change the world, a lot or a little. Not everything you want will come right away. But you are a fine person, with fine ideas, fine ideals, a fine education and fine possibilities. Keep at it, and eventually your dreams will come true.

But there's another lesson in the 26 rejections of Seuss's first book. Think of the regrets that those publishers must have had. Imagine going to your boss and saying, "Oh, yeah, we had a chance to be his publisher, but I didn't get it—One Fish, Two Fish, Red Fish, Blue Fish—what's the plot?" So there's Lesson 4: Take some chances in life, especially if those chances are based on higher ideals.

Be open-minded—open to new ideas, people, places, perspectives. People who are different from you, in all sorts of ways, have things to teach you, things you need to know in order to succeed in today's and especially tomorrow's world. So, next time someone offers you green eggs and ham, learn the lesson of Sam-I-Am: try 'em, and you might just like 'em.

Now let's consider *The Cat In The Hat*. It's probably Seuss's most famous book, one that he wrote as a challenge. In the mid-1950s, he learned that early childhood primers on reading were so, well, dull, because they had to use a prescribed vocabulary of a couple hundred words, and textbook authors didn't think that anything interesting could be written with such a restricted vocabulary. On a challenge from his publisher to write a best-seller for first-graders using only a list of 225 different words, Dr. Seuss wrote *The Cat In The Hat*. He proved that reading could be fun. And *The Cat In The Hat* became his second-best selling book of all time (the best seller? *One Fish, Two Fish, Red Fish, Blue Fish*). He followed that up with *Green Eggs and Ham*, that used only 54 words. So, there's Lesson 5: Things don't have to be hard to be good or important. Students in FW 221 know that—I hope. Life should be a joy, not a struggle. If you aren't having fun, you are doing it wrong!

I know you expect me to talk about *The Lorax*. I'm an environmental scientist, after all, and *The Lorax* is Dr. Seuss' environment book. Like the book's main character, I should speak for the trees, too. *The Lorax* is okay, but it is far from my favorite Seuss book. It's not even my favorite Seuss conservation book. It is also misunderstood. Most people think that it's an anti-logging book. But it isn't. Seuss said so himself, noting that "*The Lorax* doesn't say lumbering is immoral. I live in a house made of wood and write books printed on paper. It's a book about going easy on what we've got. It's anti-pollution and anti-greed." So, you see, Dr. Seuss is really a conservationist, in the true vision of the sustainability we talk about today. We should live today so future generations can live as they wish. That's Lesson 6: It isn't bad to use nature, it's impossible not to use nature. But take it easy, and leave some for my grandchildren and yours.

If *The Lorax* isn't my favorite, which Dr. Seuss book is? There are a lot of contenders. Like *The Sneetches*. The various stories in *The Sneetches* comprise the best overall philosophy text ever. The title story, "The Sneetches," teaches us to respect and like people different than us, however many stars they have on their bellies. "The Zax" teaches us that refusing to learn and change is the surest way to become obsolete. "Pale Green Pants With Nobody Inside Them" teaches us not to fear uncertainty and risk, but to embrace it. And "Too Many Daves"—the story of "Mrs. McDade who had 23 sons and named them all Dave"—well, it's just fun (remember Lesson 6).

But, without question, my favorite is *Scrambled Eggs Super*. You might not be familiar with this one. It's about a boy—Peter T. Hooper—who makes the greatest scrambled eggs ever by gathering eggs of the most wonderful and peculiar birds from around the wacky world of Seuss-dom. I love the book because my wife, Sharon, gave it to me in honor of our tradition of making our own scrambled-egg-super dishes on special days (albeit with only chicken eggs).

I also love it because it celebrates the diversity of nature. All those magnificent birds laying all those magnificent eggs in all sorts of magnificent places and ways. But it is also a conservation book—about biodiversity and the opportunity it provides us to experience the wonders of nature—whether we eat them or not. So, Lesson 7: Get out there and enjoy the natural world around you. Doesn't matter if you are gawking at the glory of the Grand Canyon or smiling at the insistent singing of a mockingbird. Be aware of the erratic flight of a swallowtail butterfly, or the gentle beauty of a dogwood in bloom, or the gurgling rhythm of a stream—like Rocky Branch Creek that I walked along on campus at lunchtime today. Squeeze a little nature into every day, and nature will drive away some of your problems.

Now I could go on for a long time—75 minutes is my usual program—about the wonderful lessons from Dr. Seuss. But I'm not going to do that. Instead, I'm going to end as Dr. Seuss would, with a poem. Here goes.

To You Cats in Your Hats

We wear lots of hats from
Day one to day last.
There are hats in your future,
And hats from your past.
Red hats, and green hats
And purple hats, too.
But never, no, never
A hat that's light blue!

We start with a bonnet
Knitted by grandma
And go on to chapeaus
That we wear just for glamour.
A beret as a Girl Scout
A wide brimmed beanie for baseball
And when you played cowboy,
A Stetson that stood
at least ten gallons tall.

A fez or a turban
May fit on your head.
A veil of white lace
For the day that you wed.
A Smoky Bear hat when
You become a state trooper.
Or a bizarre fascinator
That looks super-dooper!
A crown isn't likely,
But perhaps a sombrero.

Try on a thinking cap and,
Oh, the places you'll go!

Some hats will be hard
Like for deep-sea exploring.
Some will cover your ears
When the boss you're ignoring.
A skull-cap will warm you
When you're flying aloft.
Some, like your ball caps,
You might never take off.
And soon you'll be wearing
Red hats that are square
With tassels of white
Tangled up in your hair
That prove in your head
There is more there than air!

Over your life
Lots of hats you will wear.
Keep trying on new ones,
From here and from there.
You will find the right hat
That brings joy to you.
Maybe purple or green,
Yes, perhaps even blue.
It'll fit on your head
And your heart and soul, too.

So, now I'll retire
My professorial cap

'Cause it's getting late,
And I need a nap.
And now as you go
And do what you'll do,
Please never forget—
To your own hat be true!

References

1.William A. Link. 1995. William Friday: Power, purpose, and American higher education. The University of North Carolina Press, Chapel Hill, NC 494 pages. Quote page 58.

2.Ibid, page 188.

3.Ibid, page 37.

4.The Technician, October 2, 1968, North Carolina State University

5.Blog of the NC State Alumni Association, January 30, 2014

6.Ibid

7.Morris, John. 2009. Reader's Corner: 29 years Late, a Dream is Realized. 2009, by John Morris. Goodnight Raleigh. Available at: http://goodnightraleigh.com/2009/06/readers-corner-29-years-later-a-dream-is-realized/.

8.Dunn, Ian F. G. 2013. Raleigh, Then and Now: Nehi Bottling Company. Goodnight Raleigh, 01/22/2013. Available at: http://goodnightraleigh.com/2013/01/raleigh-then-and-now-nehi-bottling-company/.

9.North Carolina Highway Historical marker Program. N.C. State Fair, 1873-1925/State Exposition of 1884/ Camp Polk, 1918. NC Department of Cultural Resources. Available at: http://www.ncmarkers.com/Markers.aspx?MarkerId=H-34.

10.Hill, Michael. 2006. North Carolina Exposition of 1884. NCpedia. Available at: https://www.ncpedia.org/north-carolina-exposition-1884.

11.Wilkinson, Laura. 2010. Eduring through the decades; Historic Hillsborugh Street tavern to receive possible facelift. The Technician, Aug 29, 2010. Available at: http://www.technicianonline.com/arts_entertainment/article_c5afe240-85a0-563f-b96e-12c290a793c2.html.

ACKNOWLEDGMENTS

I would like to thank all the wonderful NC State students, staff and faculty with whom I worked for 17 years. In particular, I thank the individuals I interviewed for this collection of stories; I shared lunch with most of them, adding even more to my love of NC State and its fine people. Thanks to my family members and Katie Perry, who reviewed earlier versions of these stories and kept me from making many mistakes of fact, word or judgment; the remaining mistakes are all mine. Thanks also to my friend, novelist Katy Munger, who gave me the knowledge and encouragement to self-publish—and to keep on writing.

Photo Credits

Chapter 2: Photo of Carter-Finley Stadium by SMaloney; use allowed by Creative Commons Attribution-Share Alike 3.0 Unported.

Chapter 6: Photo of marching Band, by Edward T. Funkhouser, 2013; use allowed by Creative Commons Attribution-Share Alike 3.0 Unported.

Chapter 7: Photo of E. S. King Village: University Archives Photograph Collection. Campus facilities and views (UA023.005), Special Collections Research Center at NC State University Libraries. Permission to use granted by NC State University.

ABOUT THE AUTHOR

Larry A. Nielsen is emeritus professor of natural resources at North Carolina State University. He held academic and administrative position at Virginia Tech and Penn State before moving to NC State in 2001. There he served first as dean of the College of Natural Resources and then as university Provost, before returning to the faculty in 2009. He retired as an Alumni Distinguished Undergraduate Professor in 2017. Along with more than 100 academic and professional articles, he is co-editor or co-author of three textbooks (*Introduction to Fisheries Science, Fisheries Techniques, Ecosystem Management*). He is author of two recent books, *Provost* (2013) and *Nature's Allies* (2017). Most recently he has created the website *Today in Conservation* (todayinconservation.com), which includes stories from the history of conservation and the environment for every date of the year.

Larry lives with Sharon, his wife of more than fifty years, in Cary, North Carolina.

Contact Larry by mail at 409 Victor Hugo Drive, Cary, NC 27511 or by email at lnielsen409@gmail.com.

CPSIA information can be obtained
at www.ICGtesting.com
Printed in the USA
BVHW070042270621
610166BV00004B/13